the Ultimate Illustration Collection

THE ULTIMATE ILLUSTRATION COLLECTION
Copyright © 2008 LIAONING SCIENCE AND TECHNOLOGY PRESS

Published in Asia in 2008 by
Page One Publishing Pte Ltd

Edited and Distributed in Europe and Latin America by:
Index Book S.L
Consell de Cent 160, local 3
08015 Barcelona
T +34 93 454 5547 / F +34 93 454 8438
www.indexbook.com
e-mail: ib@indexbook.com

First published 2008 by Liaoning Science and Technology Press

Editor: Wang Lixia
Layout design: Wang Lixia
Cover design: Frédéric Snauwaert

ISBN 978-84-96774-50-6

All rights reserved. No part of this publication may be reproduced, stored in any retrieval system or transmitted, in any form or by any means, electronic, mechanical, photocopying, recording or otherwise, without prior permission in writing from the publisher. For information, contact Page One Publishing Pte Ltd, 20 Kaki Bukit View, Kaki Bukit Techpark II, Singapore 415956.

Printed and bound in SNP Leefung, Shenzhen, China

Contents

004 Introduction
006 Pencil, pen and ink
040 Watercolor, gouache
076 Acrylic
114 Computer art
186 Mixed media and collage
254 Contacts
256 Acknowledgements

Introduction

Nowadays, Illustration can be seen everywhere in magazines, art books, on the street, and even in the field of interior design. Illustration has been extensively applied in various areas, for example, some companies have used it in their products, advertisements and other designs. With the development and success in art and business, illustration has been endowed with a fresh meaning by some young artists. Illustration is an integral part of art for both the professionals and people engaged in the business area.

Illustration Collection contains works of 62 illustrators from all over the world and is categorized into five parts according to different illustration techniques: Pencil, pen and ink;Watercolour, gouache;Acrylic;Computer art;Mix media and collage. This valuable reference book will bring amazing visual experience and simulating inspiration to people.

Thanks for reading this book.

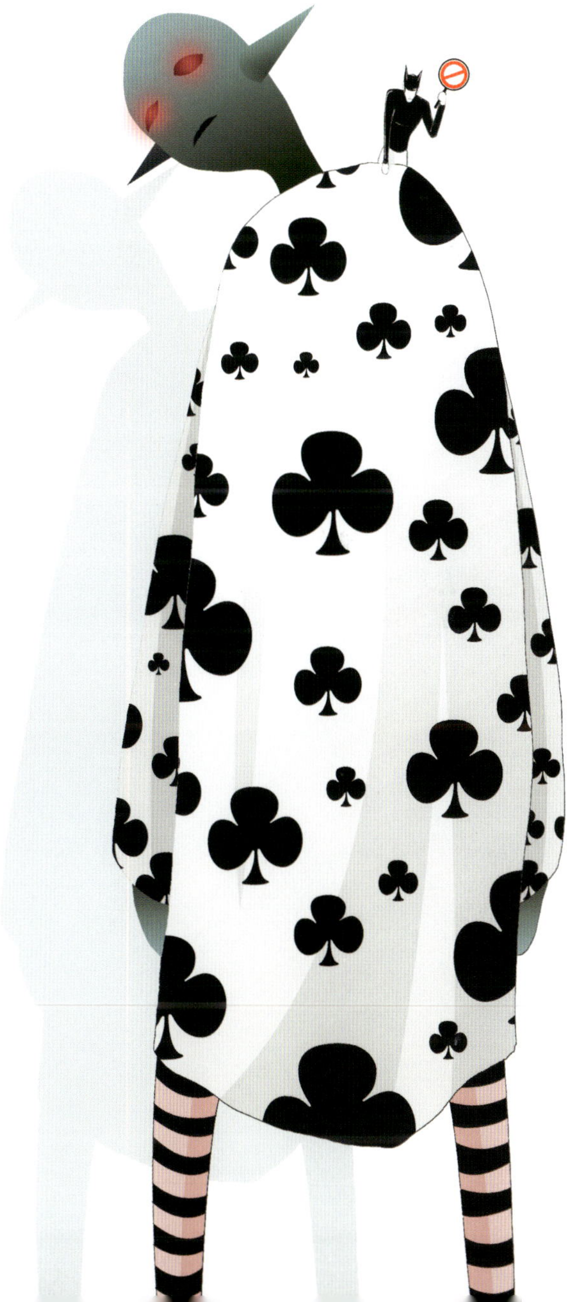

Pencil

Pen and ink

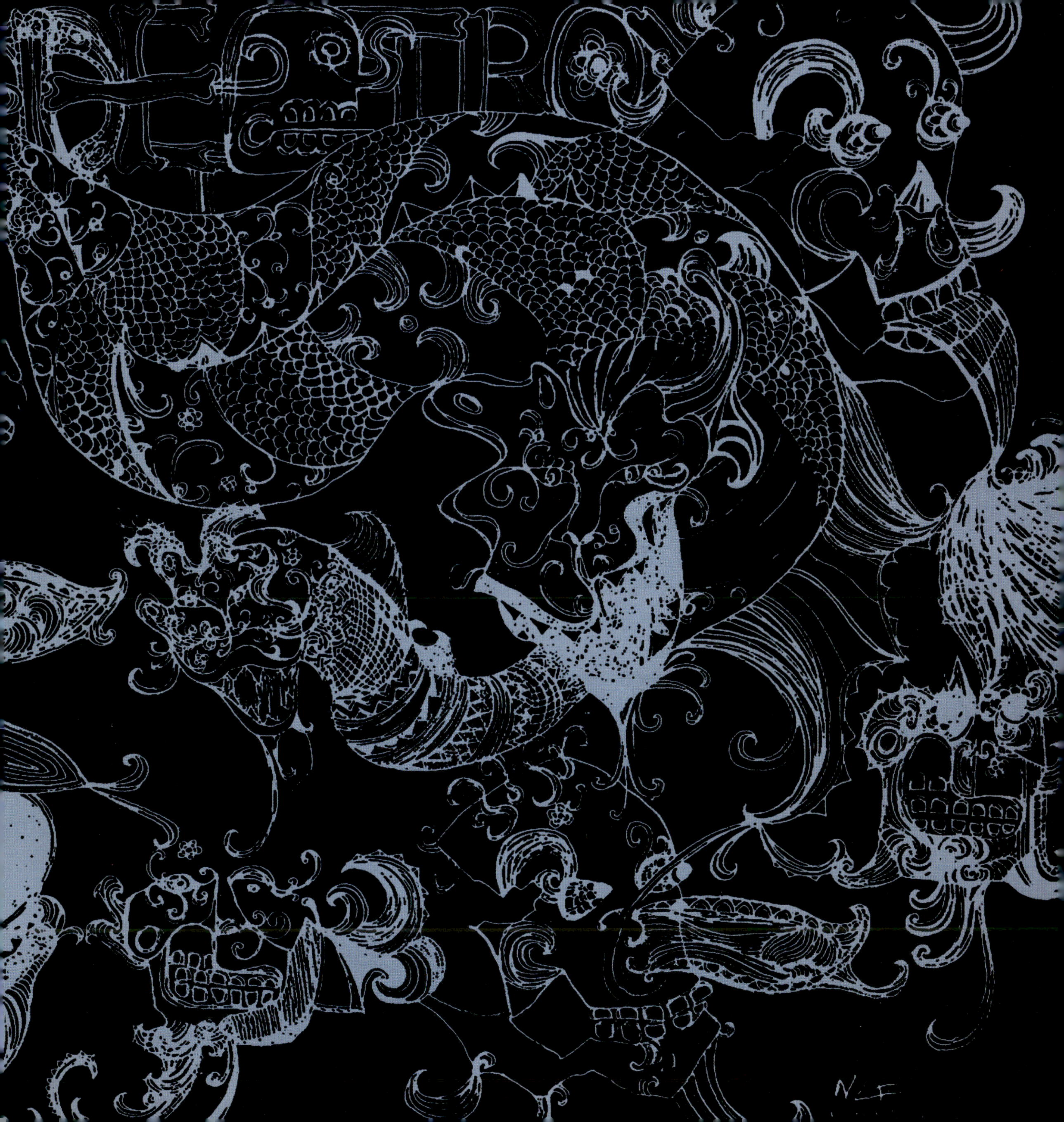

TITLE : Nothing Lasts Forever
ARTIST : Leonor Morais
COUNTRY : Portugal
MEDIUM : Pen and Ink

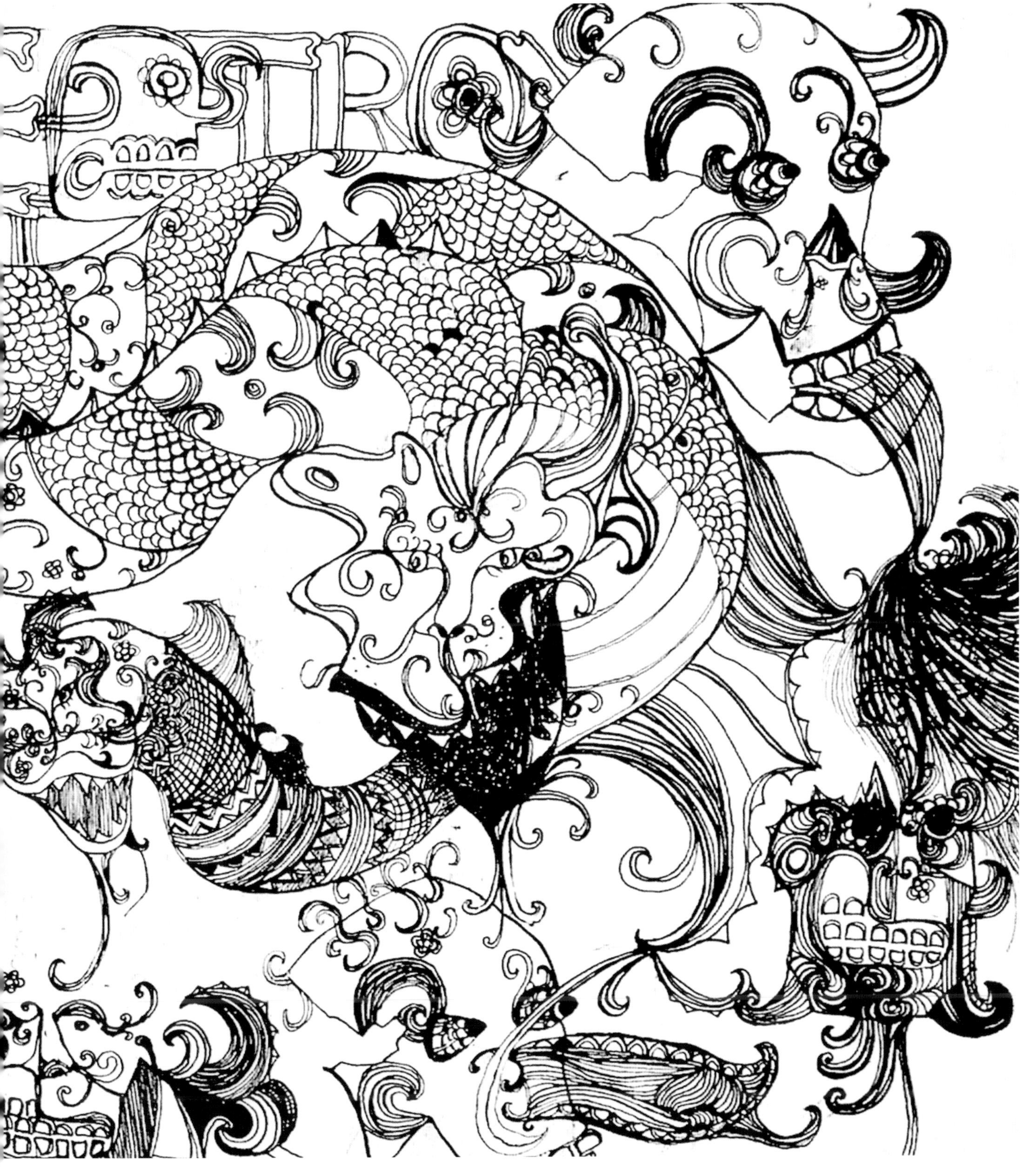

TITLE : Clinic Blossom
ARTIST : Leonor Morais
COUNTRY : Portugal
MEDIUM : Pen and Ink

011

TITLE : Depending On
ARTIST : Zhou Yijun
COUNTRY : Taiwan China
MEDIUM : Pen and Ink

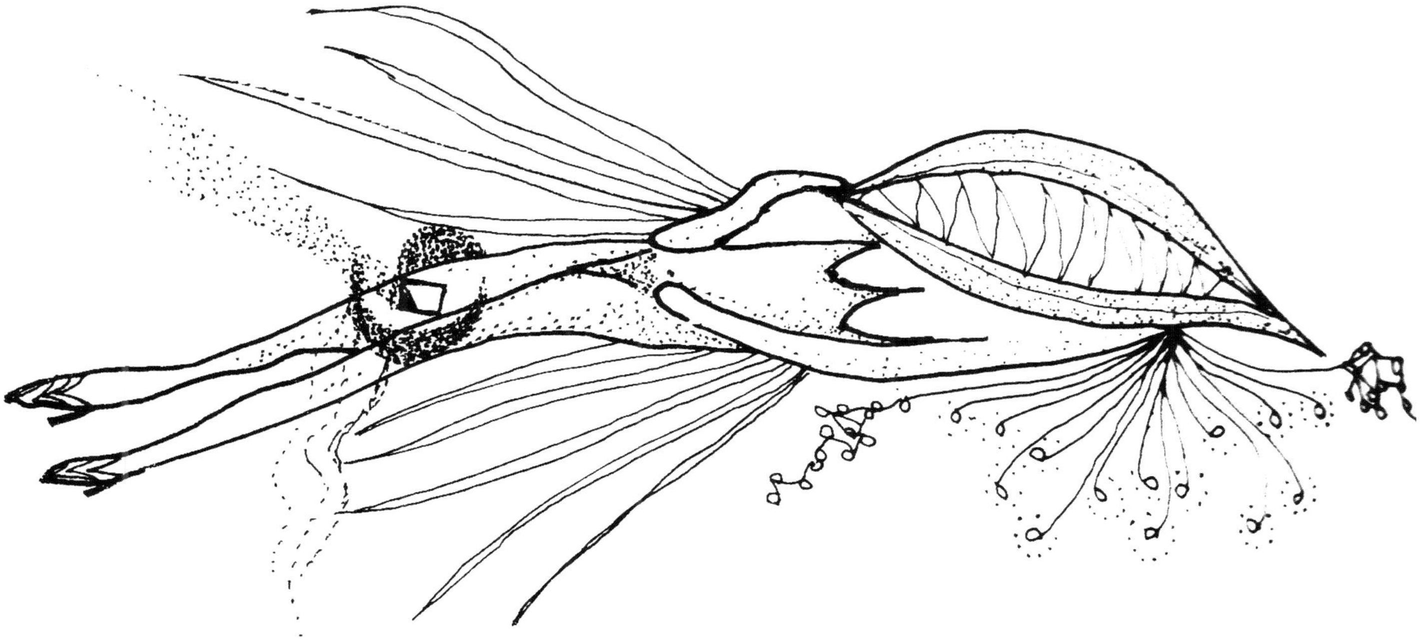

TITLE : Alice
ARTIST : Zhou Yijun
COUNTRY : Taiwan China
MEDIUM : Pen and Ink

TITLE : Love_three, is that ok?
ARTIST : Zhou Yijun
COUNTRY : Taiwan China
MEDIUM : Pen and Ink

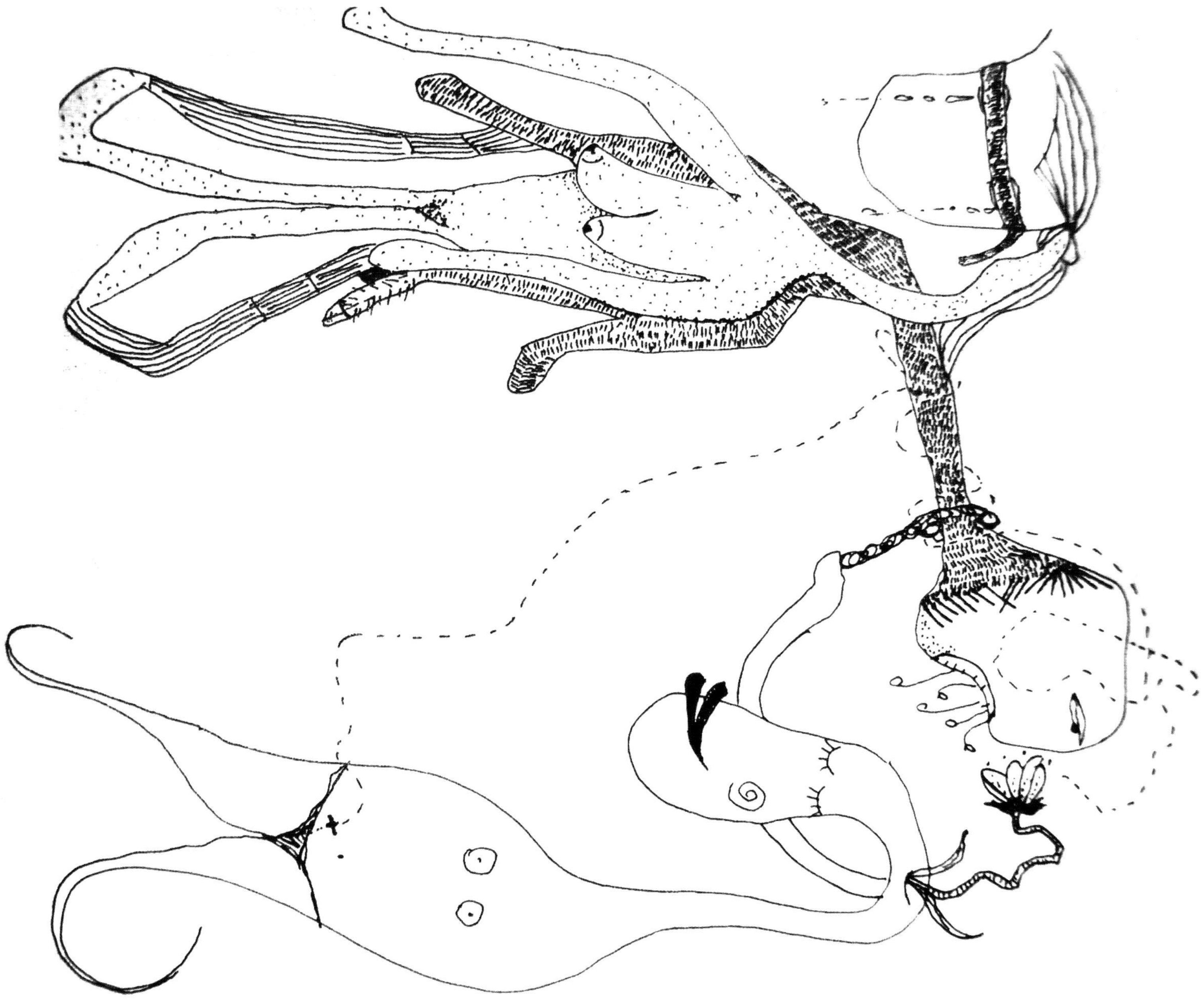

TITLE : The Girls
ARTIST : Zhou Yijun
COUNTRY : Taiwan China
MEDIUM : Pen and Ink

016

TITLE : Wipe that sound
ARTIST : Marie-Chantale Turgeon
COUNTRY : Canada
MEDIUM : Pen and Ink

017

TITLE : Memory
ARTIST : Nie Peng
COUNTRY : China
MEDIUM : Pen and Ink

TITLE : Distortion
ARTIST : Nie Peng
COUNTRY : China
MEDIUM : Pen and Ink

020

TITLE : KMC
ARTIST : Nate Smith
COUNTRY : Canada
MEDIUM : Pen and Ink

TITLE : 2th Oct.
ARTIST : Nie Peng
COUNTRY : China
MEDIUM : Pen and Ink

022

TITLE : Biblical Legends
ARTIST : Satata
COUNTRY : China
MEDIUM : Pen and Ink

TITLE : Forbidden Fruit
ARTIST : Satata
COUNTRY : China
MEDIUM : Pen and Inkr

TITLE : Rhapsody of Yeti
ARTIST : Yeji Yun
COUNTRY : Korea
MEDIUM : Pen and Ink

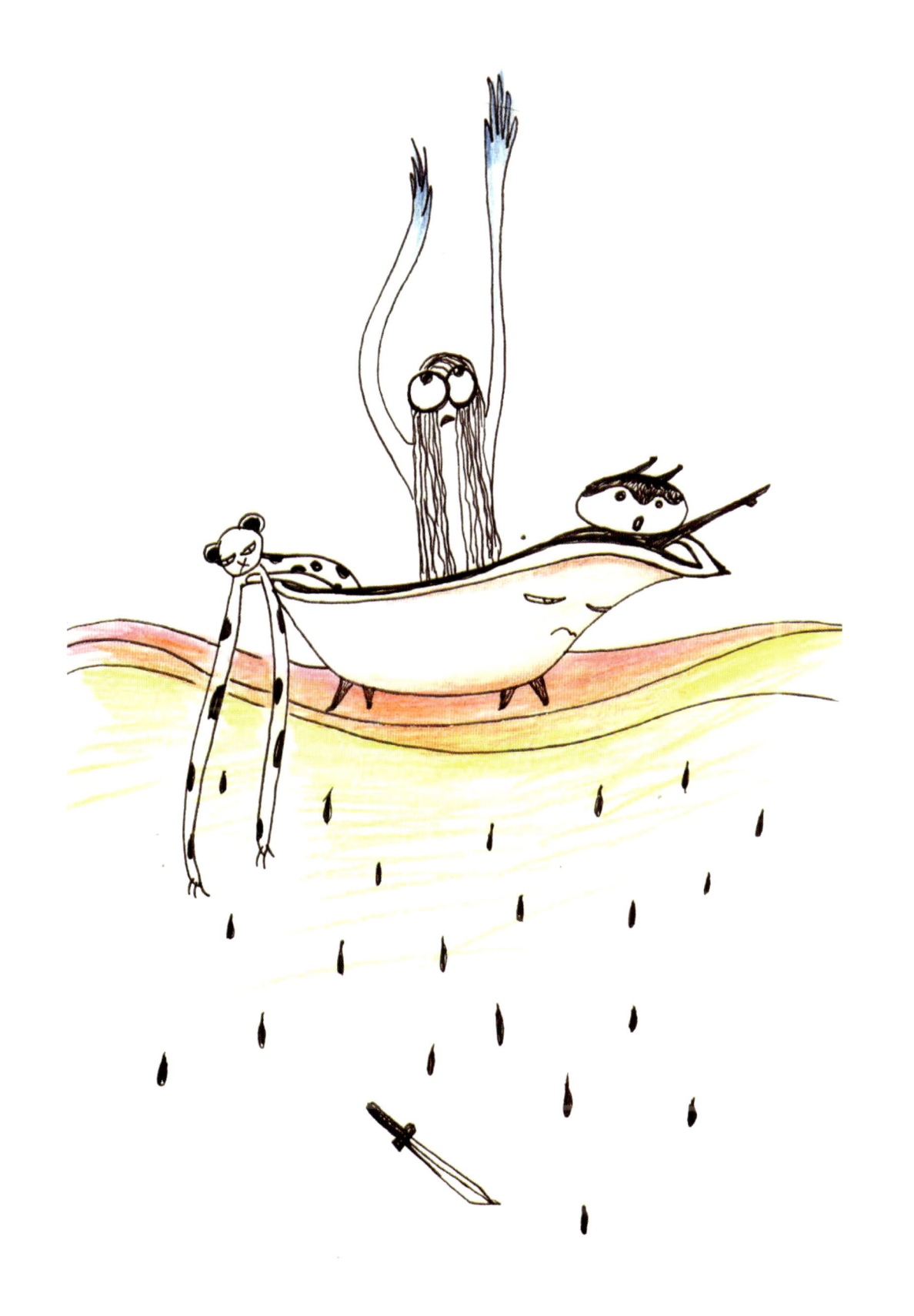

TITLE : Travels
ARTIST : Satata
COUNTRY : China
MEDIUM : Pen and Ink

TITLE : The Origin of Love
ARTIST : Yeji Yun
COUNTRY : Korea
MEDIUM : Pen and Ink

TITLE : Biblical Legends
ARTIST : Satata
COUNTRY : China
MEDIUM : Pen and Ink

TITLE : Los Amantes Del Circulo Del Polar
ARTIST : Yeji Yun
COUNTRY : Korea
MEDIUM : Pen and Ink

029

TITLE : Kids in control
ARTIST : Lodewyk M. Barkhuizen
COUNTRY : South Africa
MEDIUM : Pen and Ink

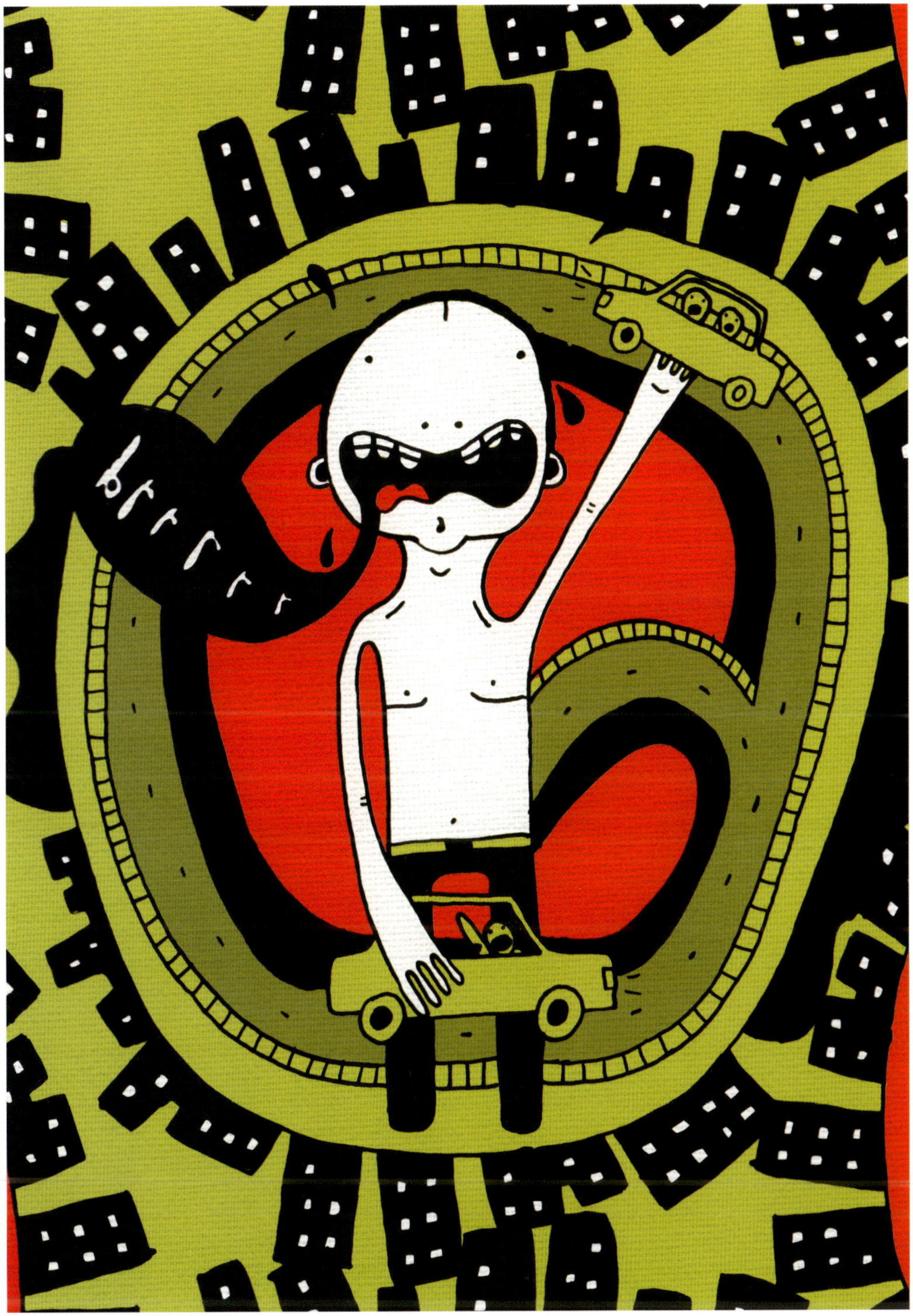
brrrrr

TITLE : Kids in control
ARTIST : Lodewyk M. Barkhuizen
COUNTRY : South Africa
MEDIUM : Pen and Ink

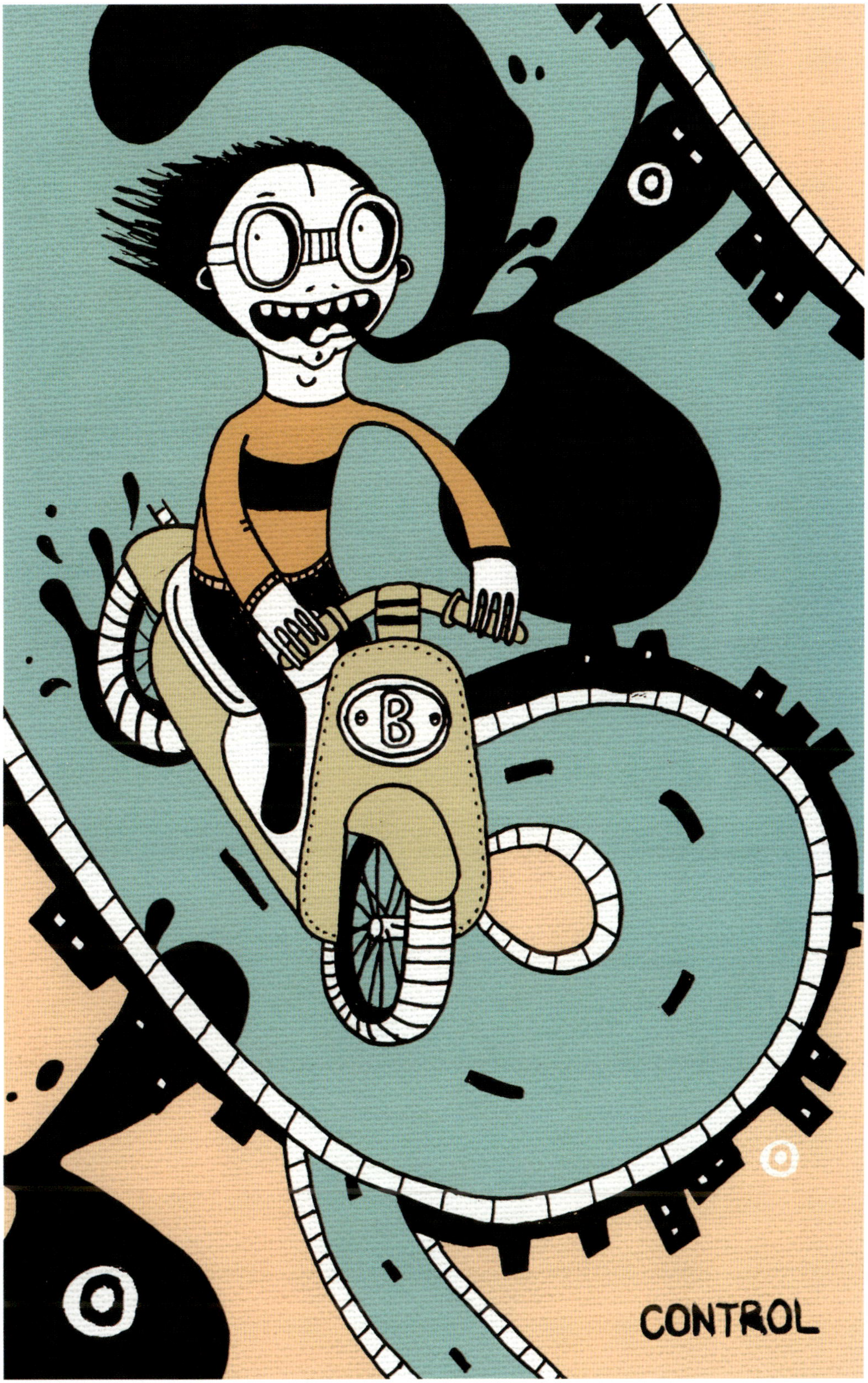
CONTROL

TITLE : Swimday
ARTIST : Lodewyk M. Barkhuizen
COUNTRY : South Africa
MEDIUM : Pen and Ink

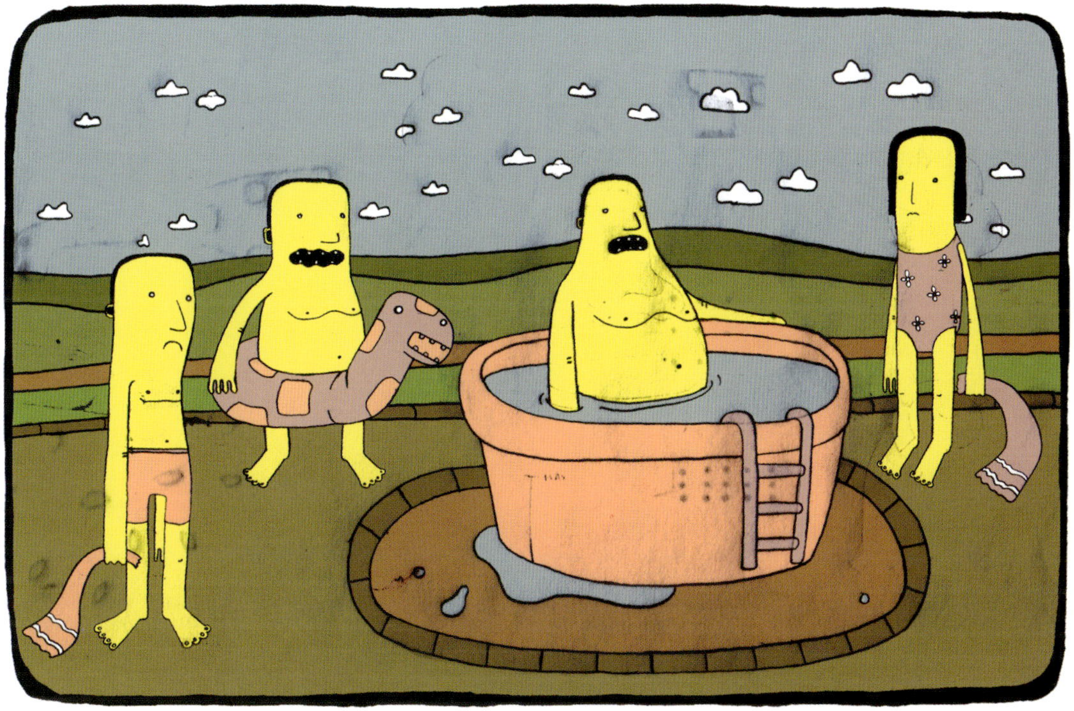

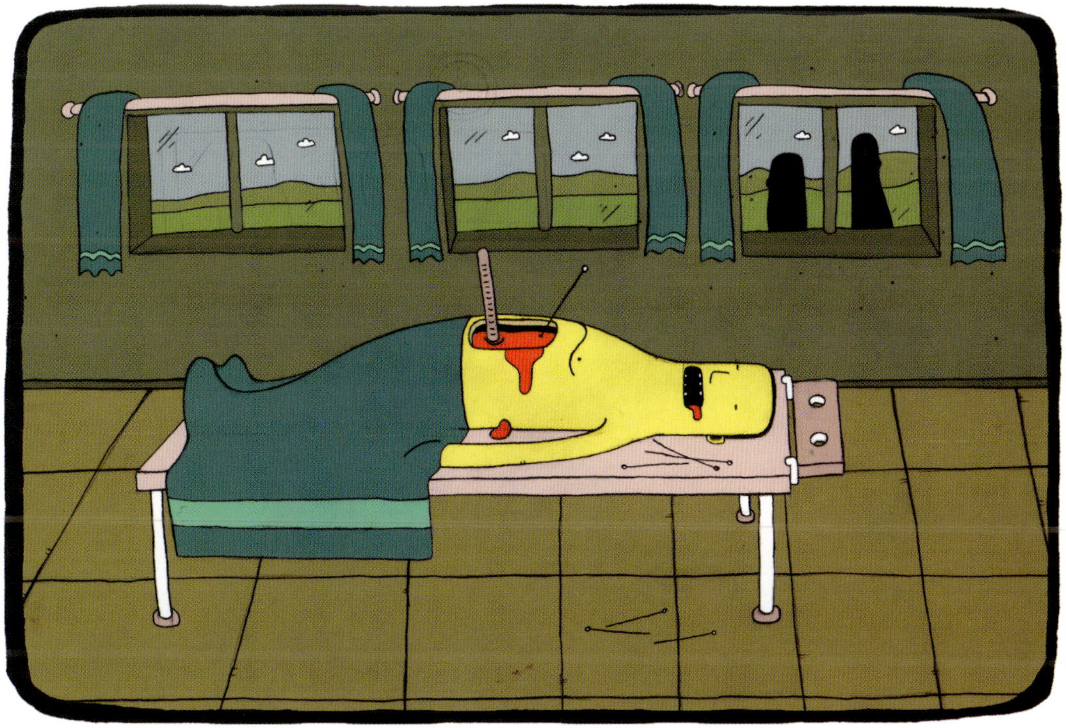

036

TITLE : Love letter
ARTIST : Yuhoo
COUNTRY : China
MEDIUM : Pen and Ink

TITLE	: Sleepwalking
ARTIST	: Ma Qiuhong
COUNTRY	: China
MEDIUM	: Pen and Ink

TITLE : You said kaka, flying balloon!
ARTIST : Yuhoo
COUNTRY : China
MEDIUM : Pen and Ink

038

TITLE : Prince, do you remember?
ARTIST : Yuhoo
COUNTRY : China
MEDIUM : Pen and Ink

Watercolour
Gouache

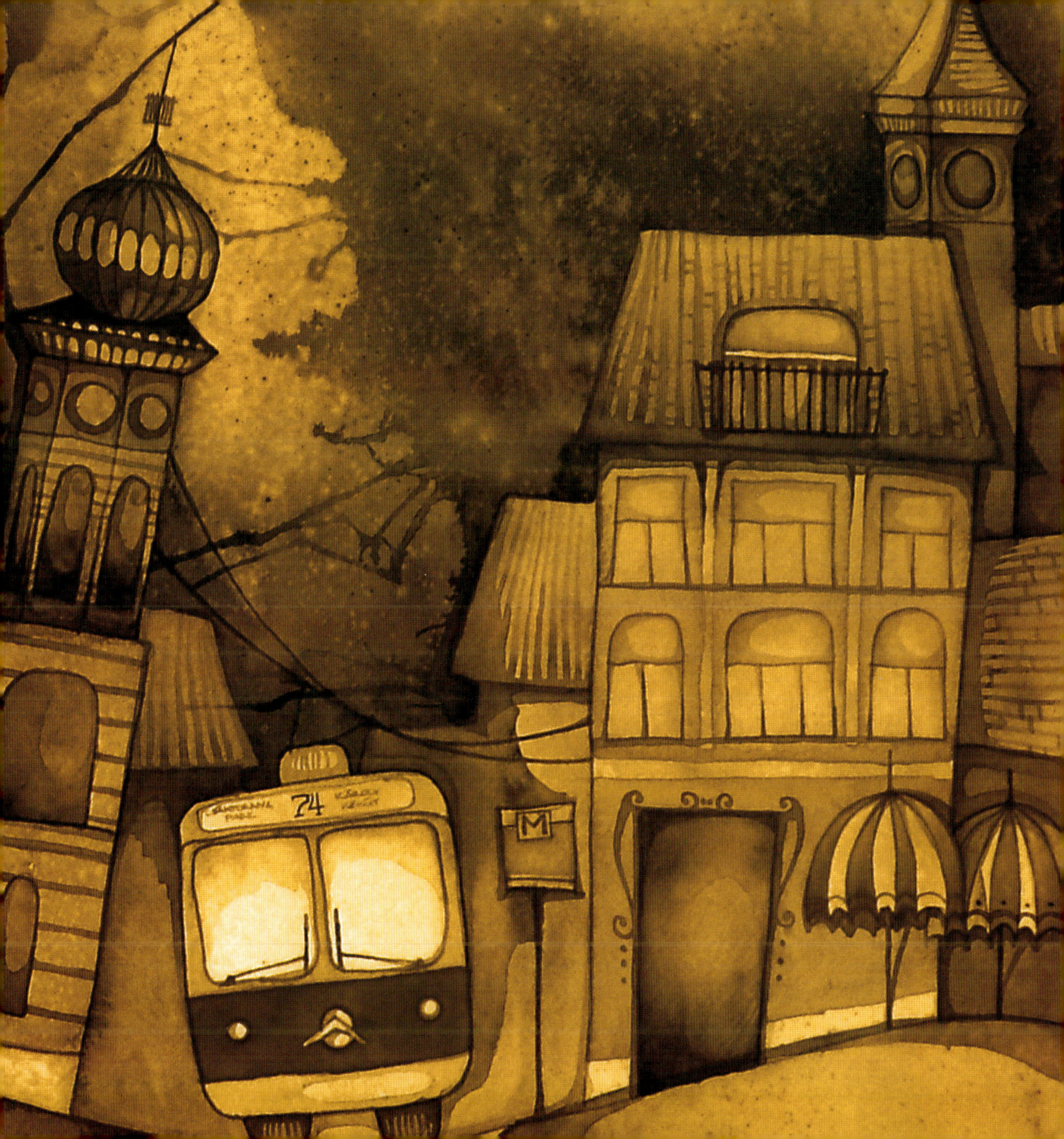
74
M

TITLE : Ng Pan and Friends
ARTIST : Postgal.com
COUNTRY : China Hongkong
MEDIUM : Watercolor

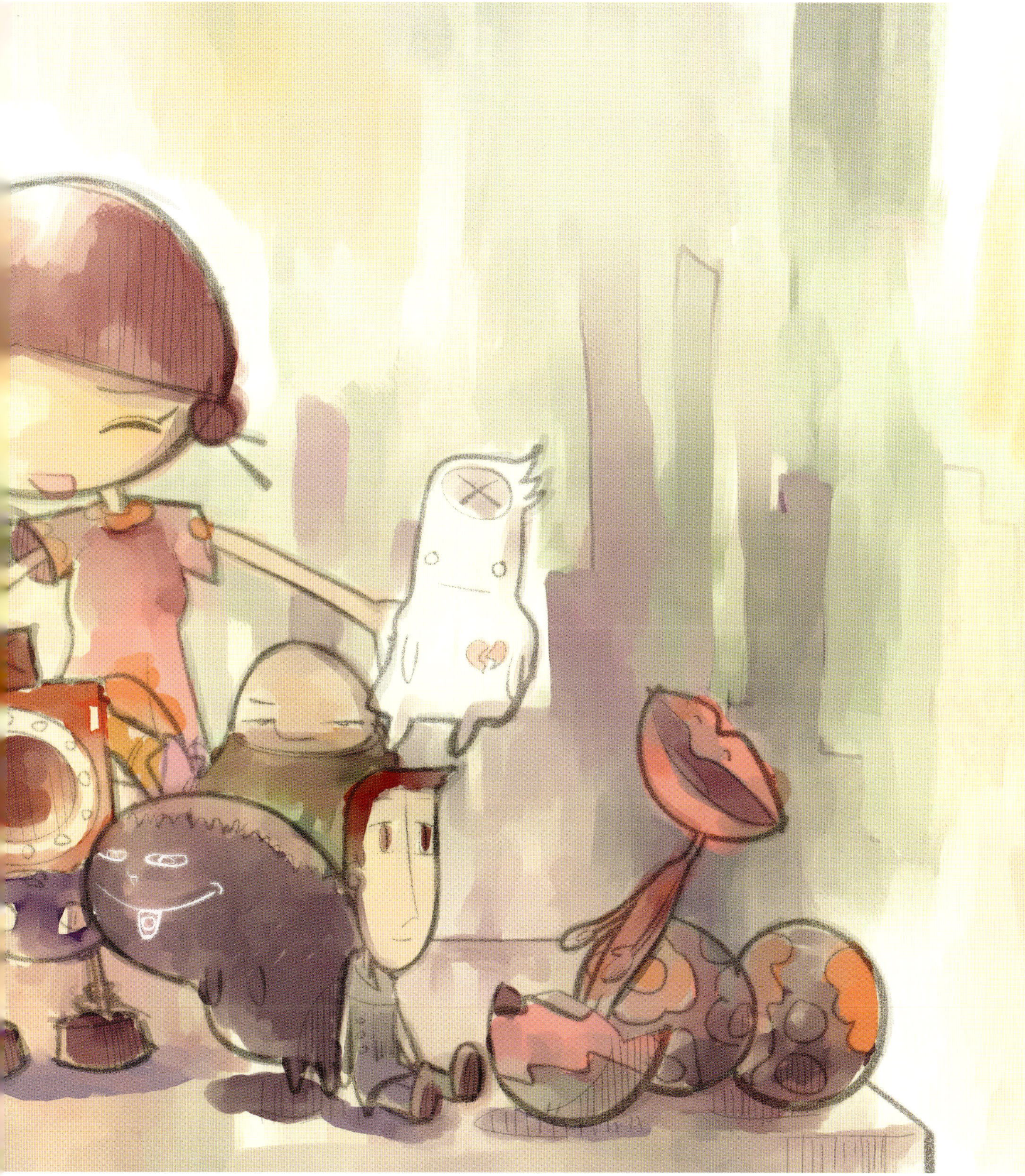

044

TITLE : Foollee, Ng Pan
ARTIST : Postgal.com
COUNTRY : China Hongkong
MEDIUM : Watercolor

045

TITLE : Grow Up, My Fafa
ARTIST : Postgal.com
COUNTRY : China Hongkong
MEDIUM : Watercolor

TITLE : Circus, Prince
ARTIST : Róth Anikó
COUNTRY : Hungary
MEDIUM : Watercolor

047

TITLE : Lady Bird
ARTIST : Róth Anikó
COUNTRY : Hungary
MEDIUM : Watercolor

TITLE : Budapest
ARTIST : Róth Anikó
COUNTRY : Hungary
MEDIUM : Watercolor

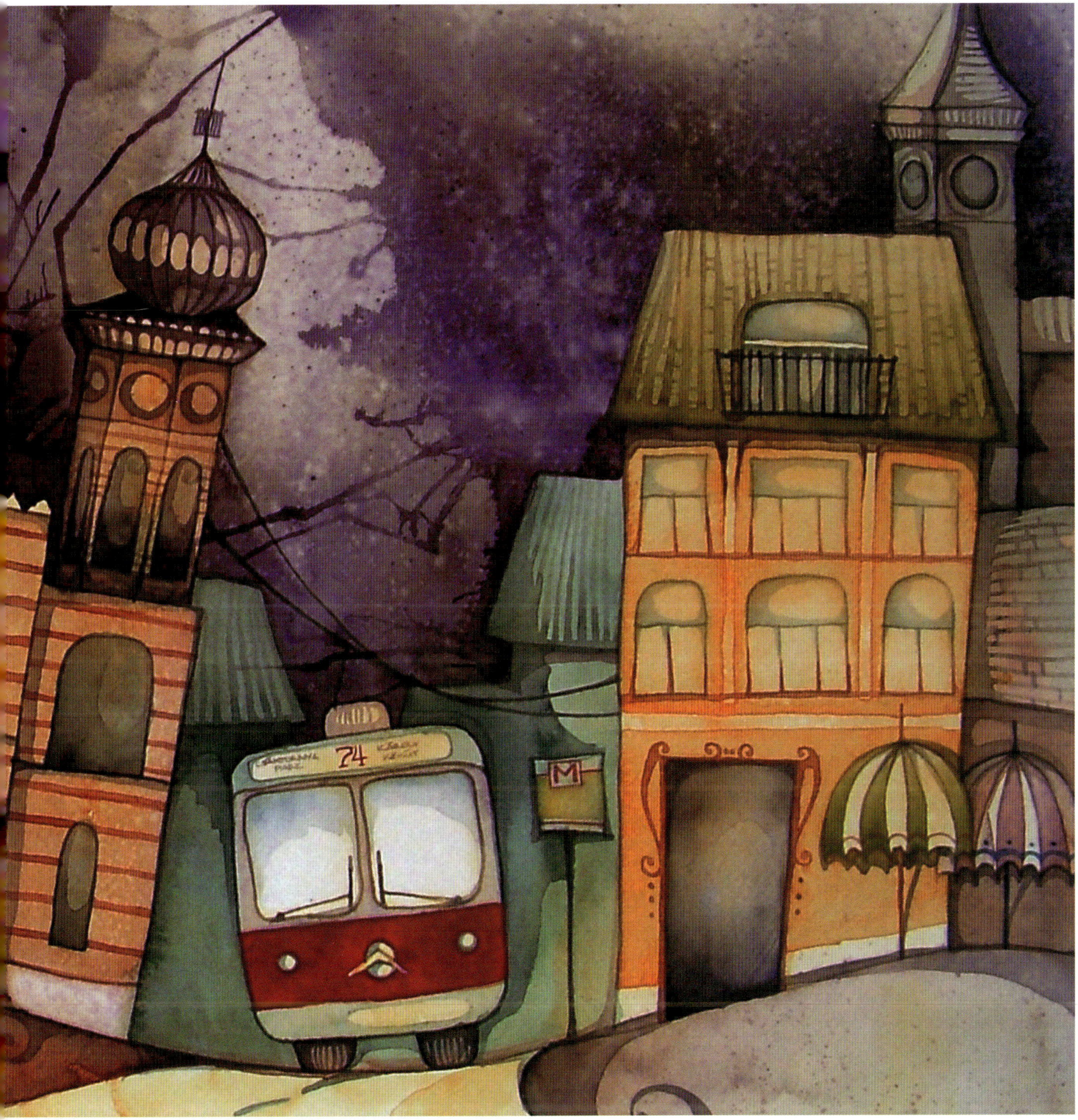
74
M

050

TITLE : Rolling_houses
ARTIST : Róth Anikó
COUNTRY : Hungary
MEDIUM : Watercolor

051

TITLE : Cat
ARTIST : Róth Anikó
COUNTRY : Hungary
MEDIUM : Watercolor

052

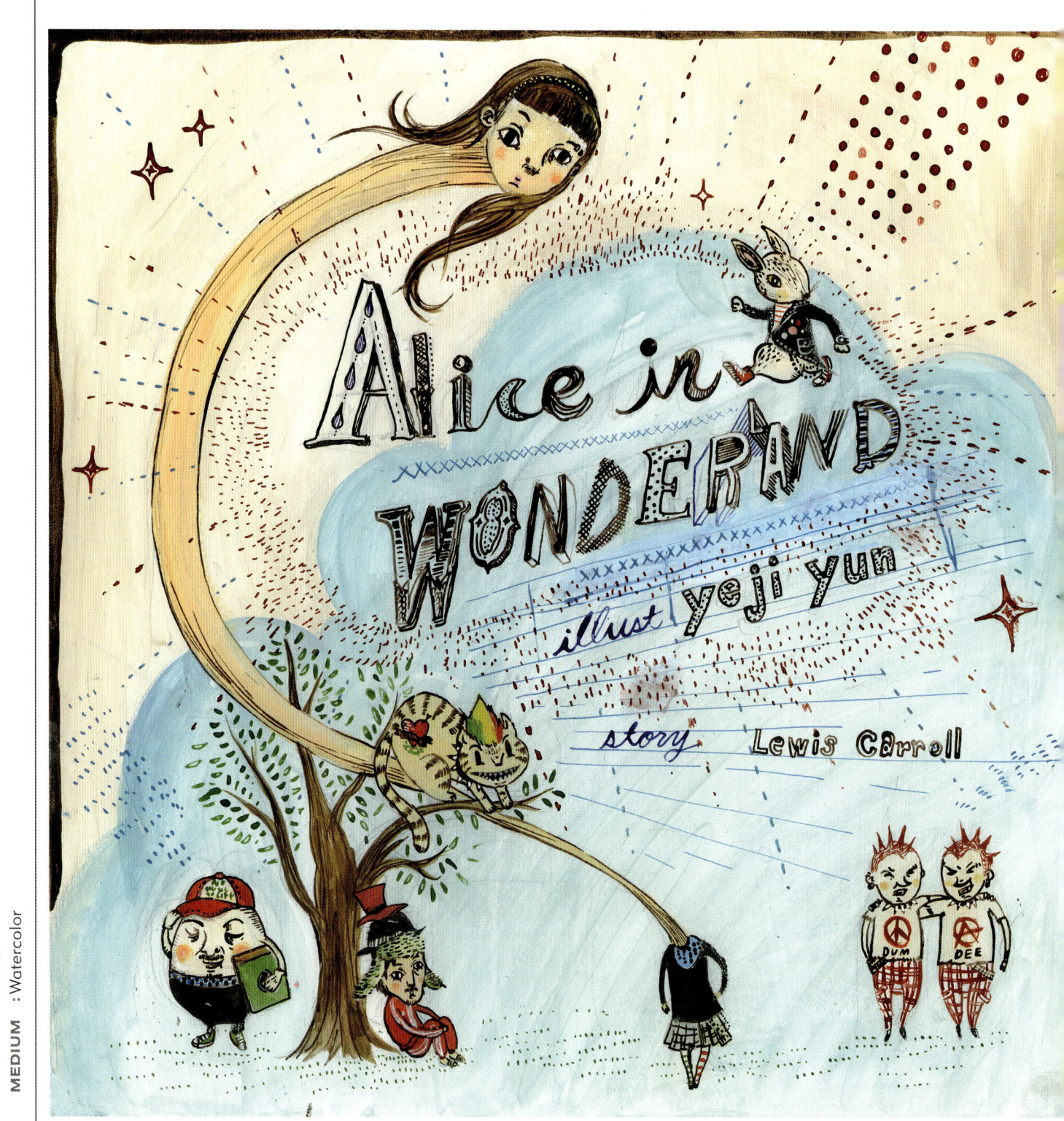

TITLE : Alice in Wonderland
ARTIST : Yeji Yun
COUNTRY : Korea
MEDIUM : Watercolor

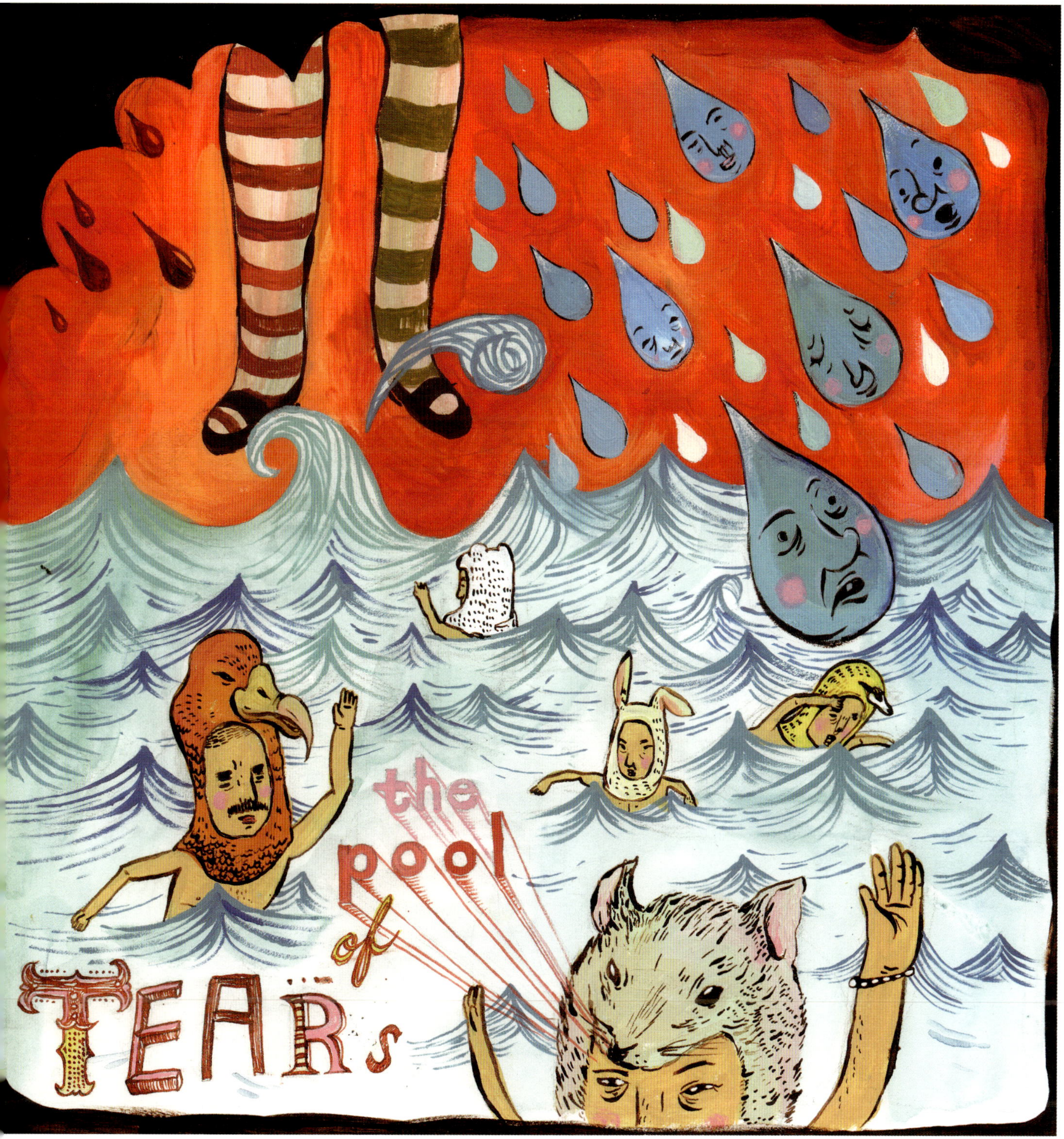
the pool of TEARs

TITLE : Alice in Wonderland
ARTIST : Yeji Yun
COUNTRY : Korea
MEDIUM : Watercolor

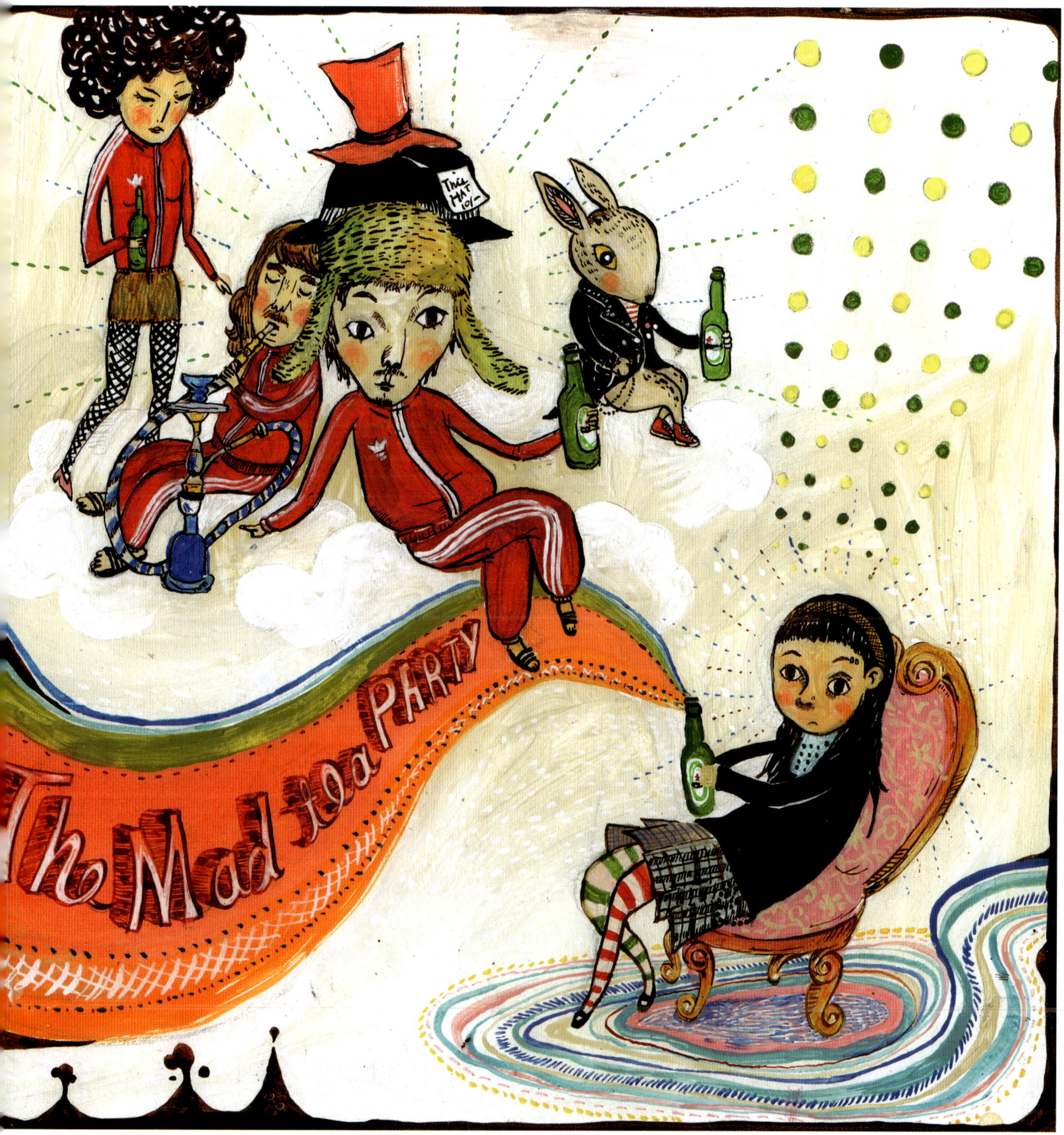
This HAT 10/-
The Mad tea PARTY

056

TITLE : Carrousel
ARTIST : Yuhoo
COUNTRY : China
MEDIUM : Gouache

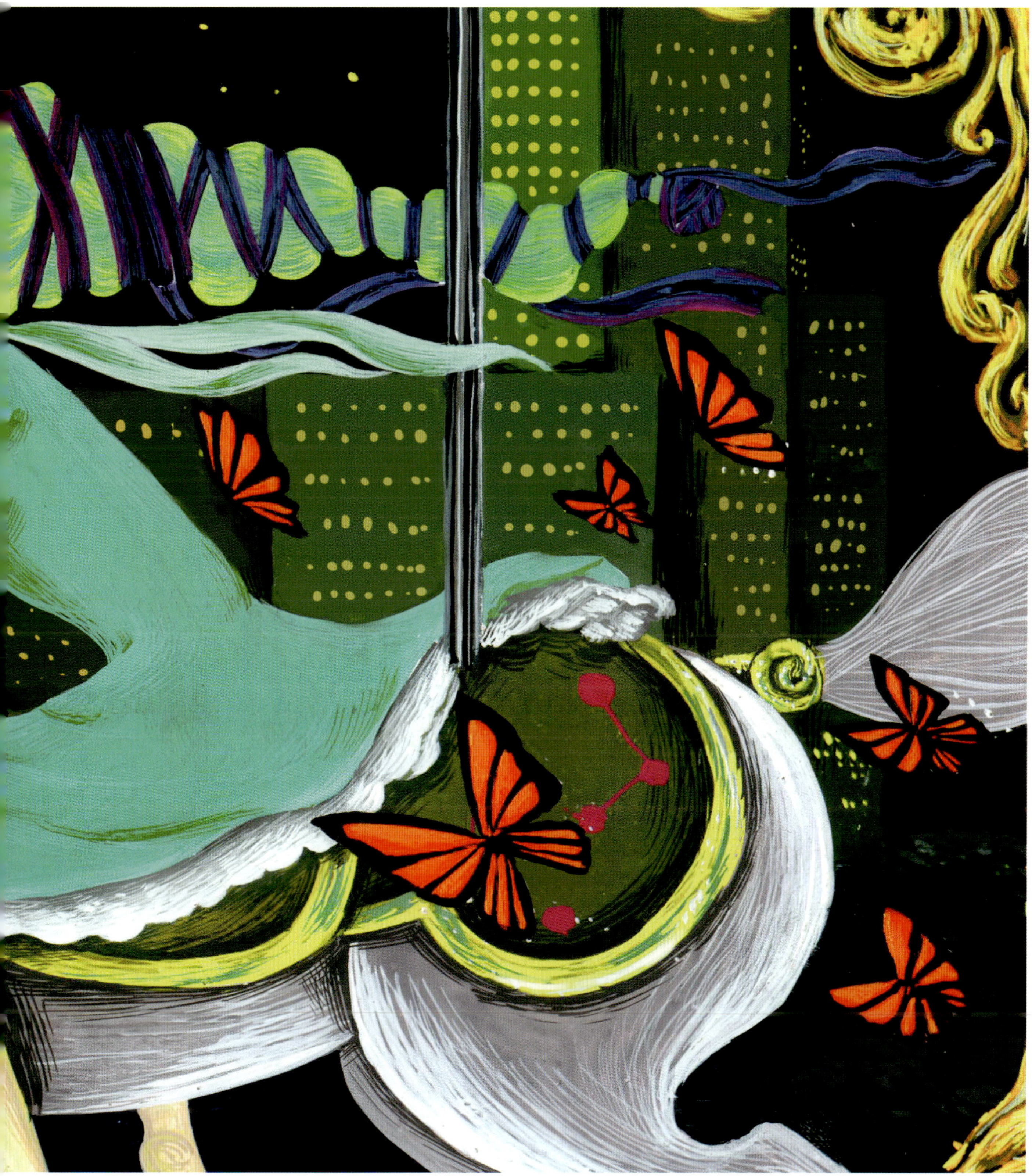

058

TITLE : Xlarge Kgard
ARTIST : Ken Garduno
COUNTRY : US
MEDIUM : Watercolor

TITLE : Lovew
ARTIST : Ken Garduno
COUNTRY : US
MEDIUM : Watercolor

060

TITLE : Envy
ARTIST : Ken Garduno
COUNTRY : US
MEDIUM : Watercolor

TITLE: Truth about man
ARTIST: Ken Garduno
COUNTRY: US
MEDIUM: Watercolor

TITLE : Magic Scarecrow
ARTIST : He Chuan
COUNTRY : China
MEDIUM : Watercolor

TITLE : Love spread
ARTIST : He Chuan
COUNTRY : China
MEDIUM : Watercolor

TITLE : Shaving
ARTIST : Ai Tatebayashi
COUNTRY : US
MEDIUM : Gouache

TITLE : Nice Shot
ARTIST : Ai Tatebayashi
COUNTRY : US
MEDIUM : Gouache

066

TITLE : Obesity
ARTIST : Ai Tatebayashi
COUNTRY : US
MEDIUM : Gouache

TITLE : Wedding Party
ARTIST : Ai Tatebayashi
COUNTRY : US
MEDIUM : Gouache

067

TITLE : Herod
ARTIST : Shin Eun-mi
COUNTRY : South Korea
MEDIUM : Watercolor

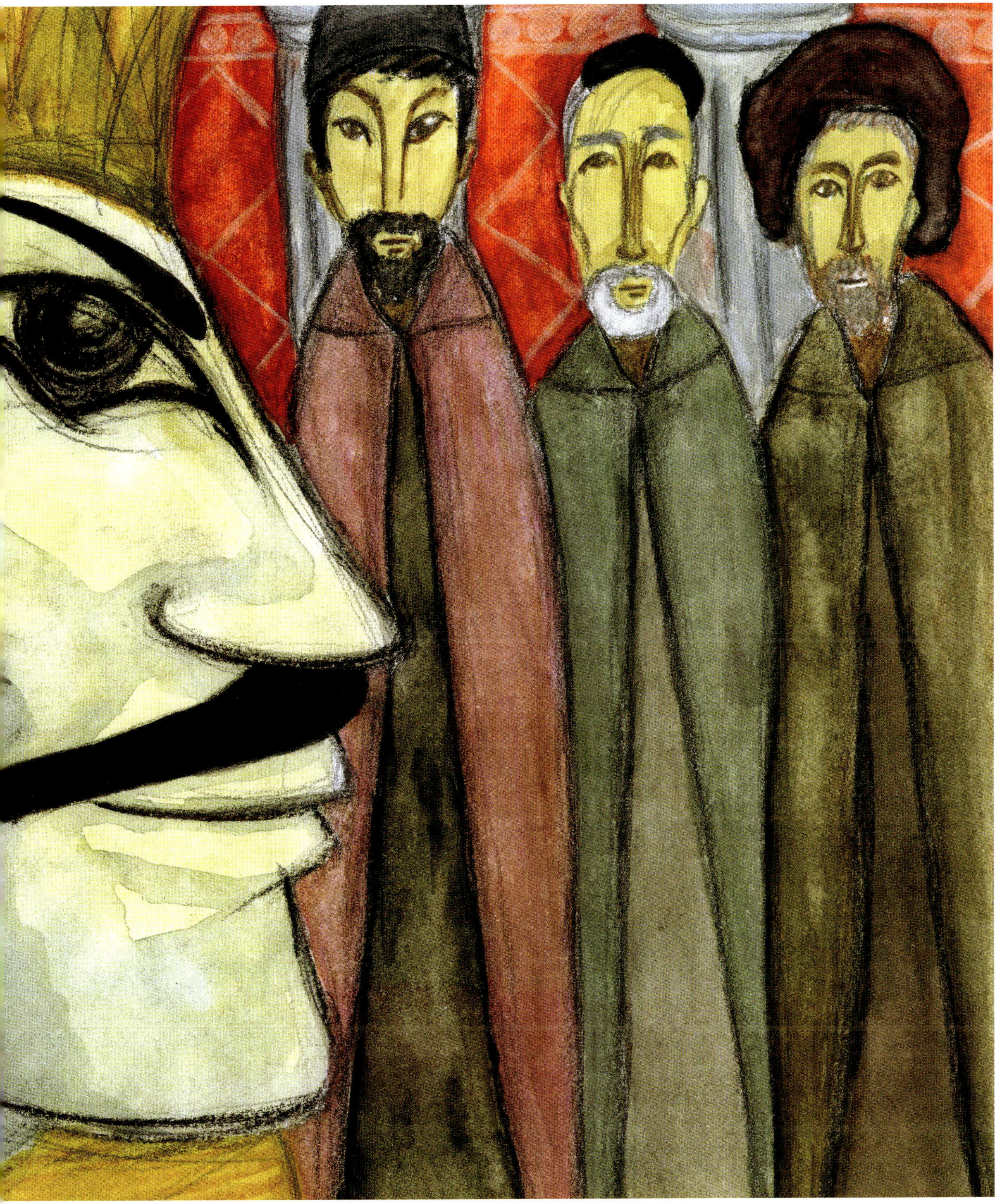

TITLE : Comfort
ARTIST : Shin Eun-mi
COUNTRY : South Korea
MEDIUM : Watercolor

TITLE : Child Right
ARTIST : Cutting Edge Design Studio
COUNTRY : US
MEDIUM : Gouache

TITLE : What shoud i do?
ARTIST : Shin Eun-mi
COUNTRY : South Korea
MEDIUM : Gouache

TITLE : A Hard Day
ARTIST : Shin Eun-mi
COUNTRY : South Korea
MEDIUM : Gouache

TITLE : Mark first
ARTIST : Shi Wuxuan
COUNTRY : China
MEDIUM : Gouache

TITLE : Where are your rails heading for?
ARTIST : Shi Wuxuan
COUNTRY : China
MEDIUM : Gouache

Acrylic

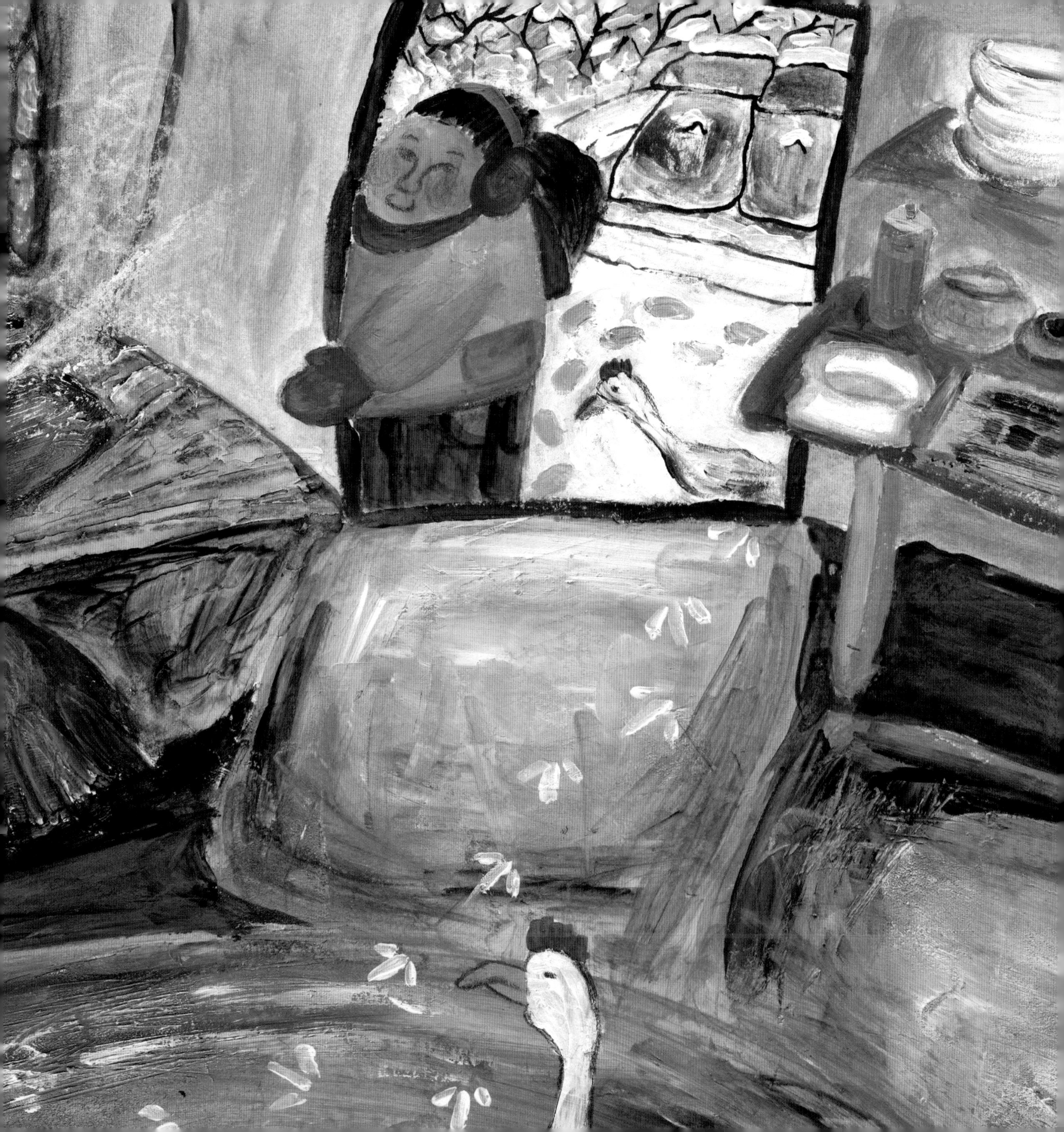

TITLE : Dimples
ARTIST : Yuhoo
COUNTRY : China
MEDIUM : Acrylic

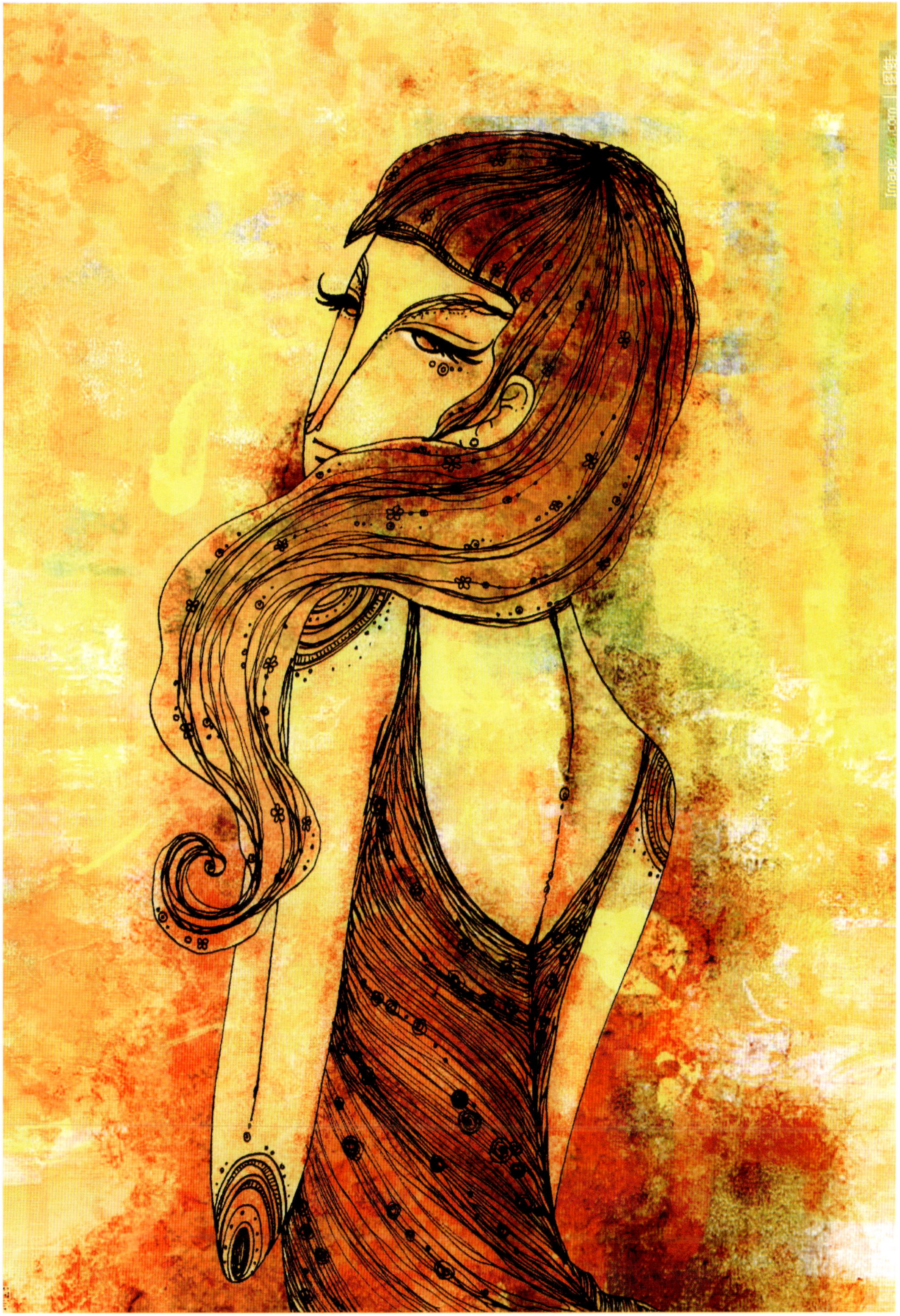

TITLE   : Designer
ARTIST : Pi Jiupaopao
COUNTRY : China
MEDIUM : Acrylic

081

082

TITLE : Maybe we could
ARTIST : Michael Foster
COUNTRY : US
MEDIUM : Acrylic

TITLE : I'm really not that anxious
ARTIST : Michael Foster
COUNTRY : US
MEDIUM : Acrylic

084

TITLE : Rest & Relaxation
ARTIST : Michael Foster
COUNTRY : US
MEDIUM : Acrylic

TITLE : The Wind Blows
ARTIST : Shin Eun-mi
COUNTRY : South Korea
MEDIUM : Acrylic

TITLE : Doodle on The Wooden Box
ARTIST : Ma Qiuhong
COUNTRY : China
MEDIUM : Acrylic

TITLE : House people
ARTIST : Ma Qiuhong
COUNTRY : China
MEDIUM : Acrylic

TITLE : Conception
ARTIST : Ma Qiuhong
COUNTRY : China
MEDIUM : Acrylic

TITLE : In the orchard
ARTIST : Ma Qiuhong
COUNTRY : China
MEDIUM : Acrylic

TITLE : Marry easily, divorce hard
ARTIST : A Moxilin
COUNTRY : China
MEDIUM : Acrylic

TITLE : Happy birthday Eighth Route Army man
ARTIST : A Moxilin
COUNTRY : China
MEDIUM : Acrylic

TITLE : Are you alone too?
ARTIST : Shi Wuxuan
COUNTRY : China
MEDIUM : Acrylic

你也是一个人？

TITLE : Blower
ARTIST : Chaos
COUNTRY : China Taiwan
MEDIUM : Acrylic

TITLE : Allure
ARTIST : Chaos
COUNTRY : China Taiwan
MEDIUM : Acrylic

TITLE : Michael Jackson
ARTIST : Brian Taylor
COUNTRY : US
MEDIUM : Oil

097

TITLE : Basement Jaxx
ARTIST : Brian Taylor
COUNTRY : US
MEDIUM : Oil

TITLE : Pop Culture Junkie
ARTIST : Brian Taylor
COUNTRY : US
MEDIUM : Oil

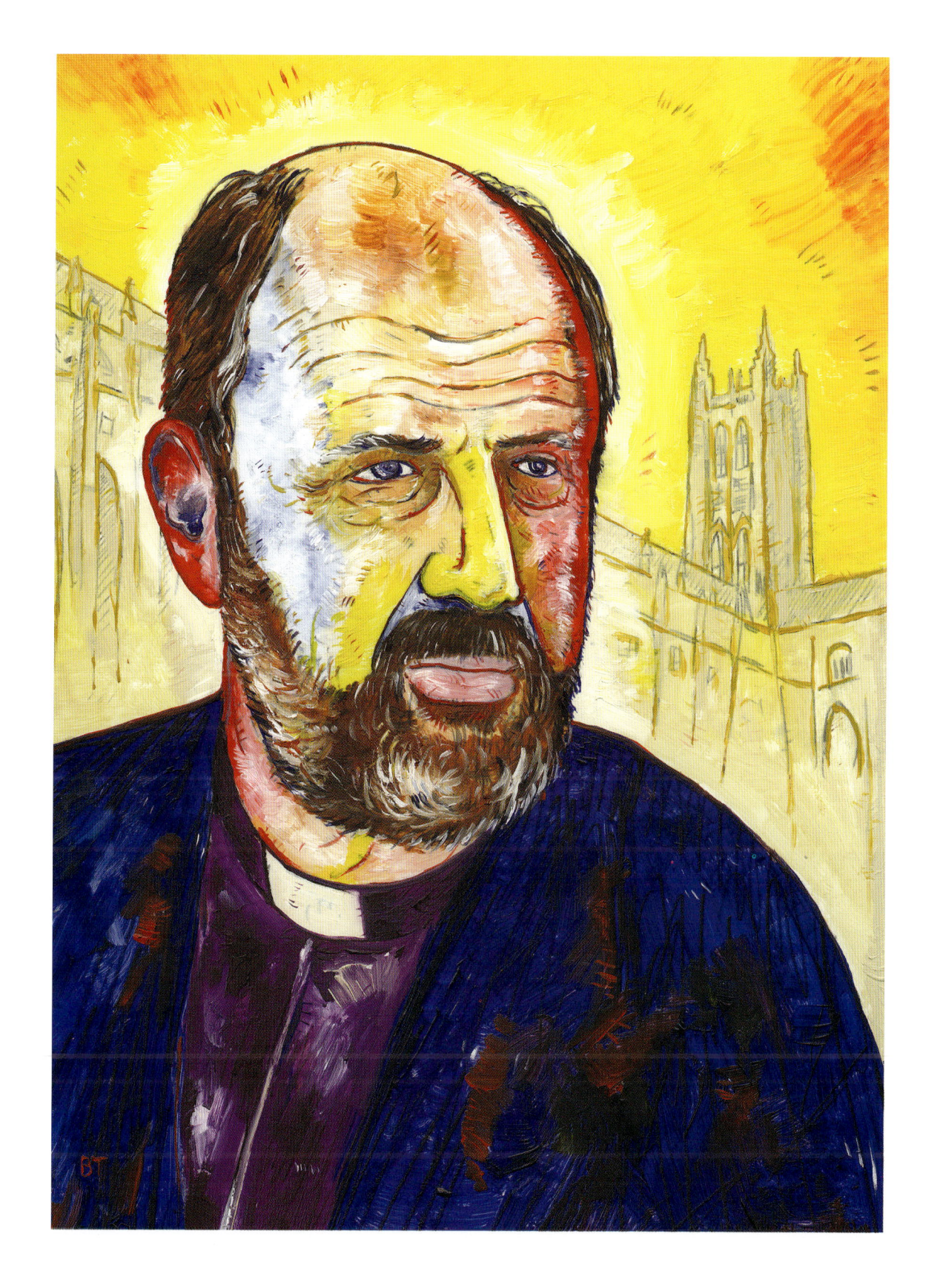

TITLE: NT Wright
ARTIST: Brian Taylor
COUNTRY: US
MEDIUM: Oil

TITLE : A Solitude
ARTIST : Shin Eun-mi
COUNTRY : South Korea
MEDIUM : Acrylic

TITLE : Oops, When Nowhere Sit In Subway
ARTIST : Shin Eun-mi
COUNTRY : South Korea
MEDIUM : Acrylic

TITLE   : The Mother of My Mother
ARTIST : Shin Eun-mi
COUNTRY : South Korea
MEDIUM : Acrylic

103

TITLE : Sweet Talk
ARTIST : Liz Amini-Holmes
COUNTRY : US
MEDIUM : Acrylic

TITLE : Fais Dodo
ARTIST : Liz Amini-Holmes
COUNTRY : US
MEDIUM : Acrylic

TITLE : Red Book
ARTIST : Liz Amini-Holmes
COUNTRY : US
MEDIUM : Acrylic

TITLE : Fall Walk
ARTIST : Liz Amini-Holmes
COUNTRY : US
MEDIUM : Acrylic

TITLE : Keane2
ARTIST : Manuel Larino
COUNTRY : Spain
MEDIUM : Acrylic

TITLE : Puzled
ARTIST : Manuel Larino
COUNTRY : Spain
MEDIUM : Acrylic

110

TITLE : My Pet Boy
ARTIST : Ma Qiuhong
COUNTRY : China
MEDIUM : Acrylic

TITLE : Love Books
ARTIST : Liz Amini-Holmes
COUNTRY : US
MEDIUM : Acrylic

TITLE : 1000 Teddies
ARTIST : Philipp Jordan
COUNTRY : The Netherlands
MEDIUM : Acrylic

113

Computer art

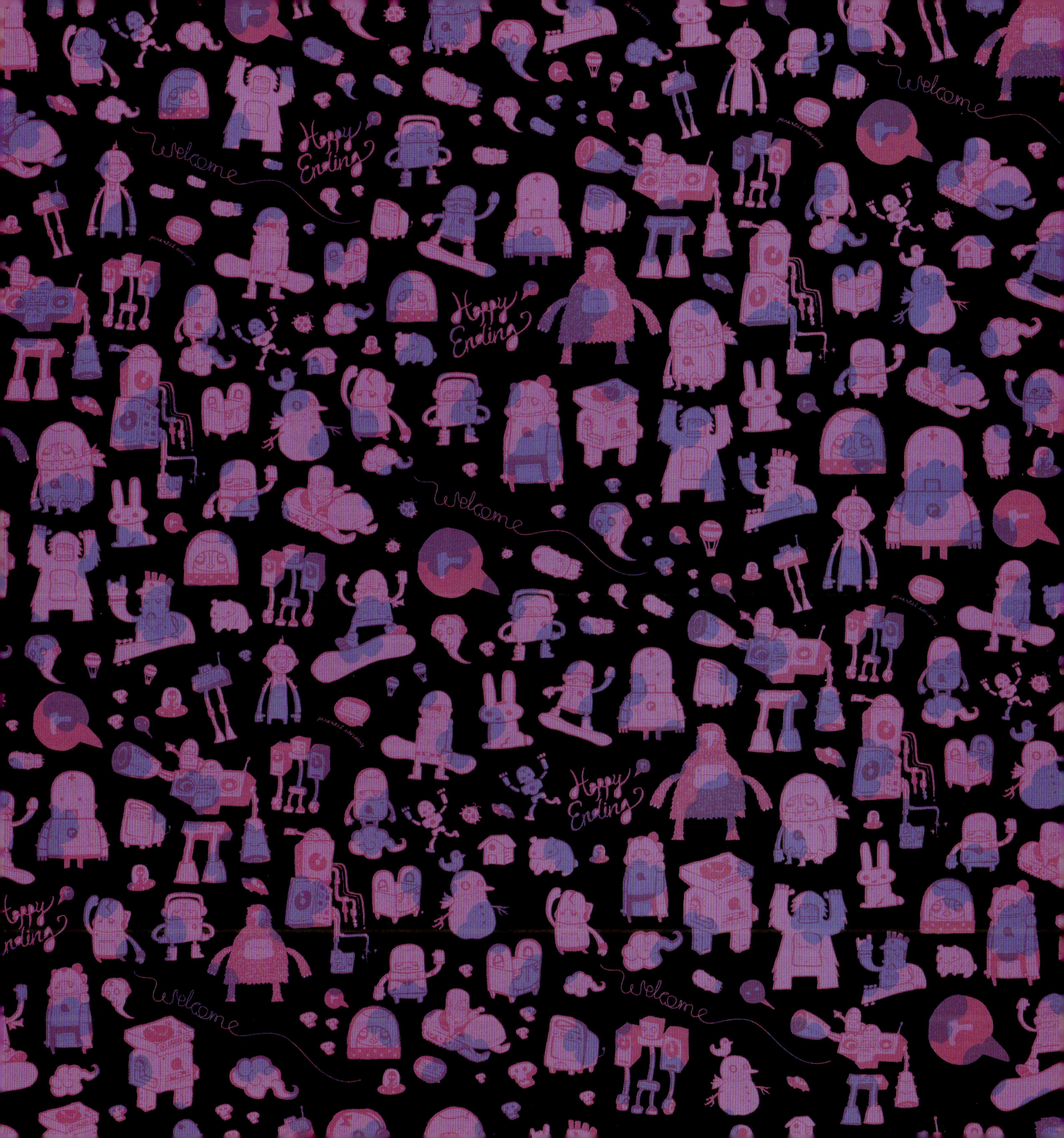
Welcome
Happy Ending

TITLE : Doll-doll.com
ARTIST : Postgal.com
COUNTRY : Hong Kong
MEDIUM : Vector [Computer Graphics]

117

TITLE : Super Bastard Box Art Character
ARTIST : Undoboy
COUNTRY : US
MEDIUM : Vector [Computer Graphics]

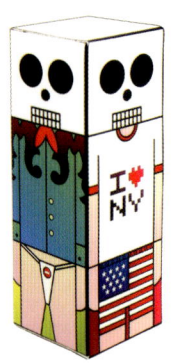

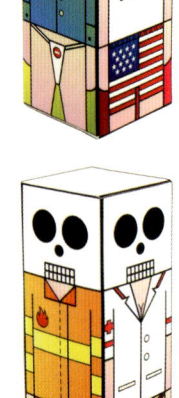

119

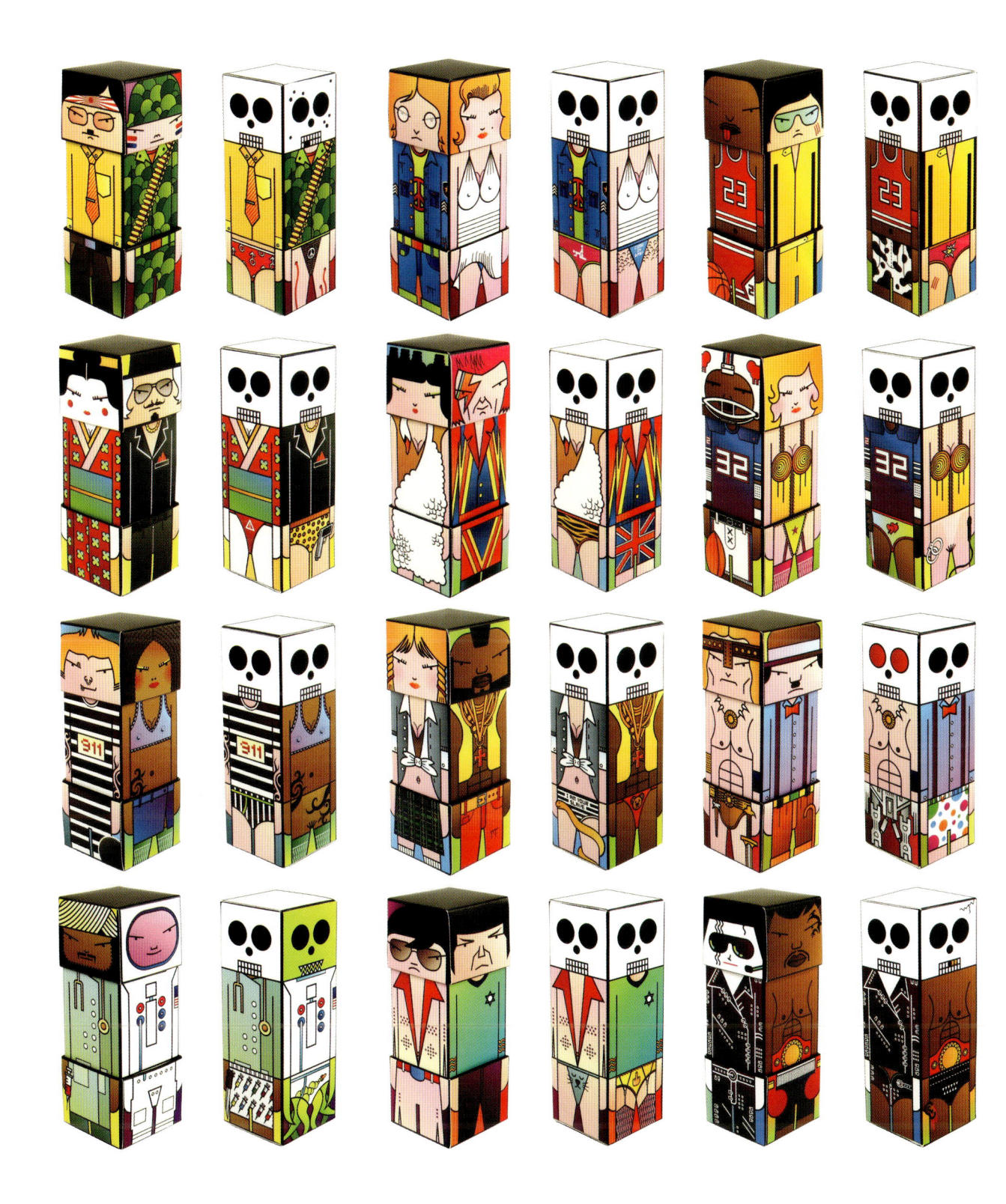

TITLE : 3D Rat
ARTIST : Ippei Gyoubu
COUNTRY : Japan
MEDIUM : Vector [Computer Graphics]

TITLE : Abriendo Caminos
ARTIST : Gustavo Torres & Clara Luzian
COUNTRY : Argentina
MEDIUM : Vector [Computer Graphics]

TITLE : 10 Monkeys
ARTIST : Ippei Gyoubu
COUNTRY : Japan
MEDIUM : Vector [Computer Graphics]

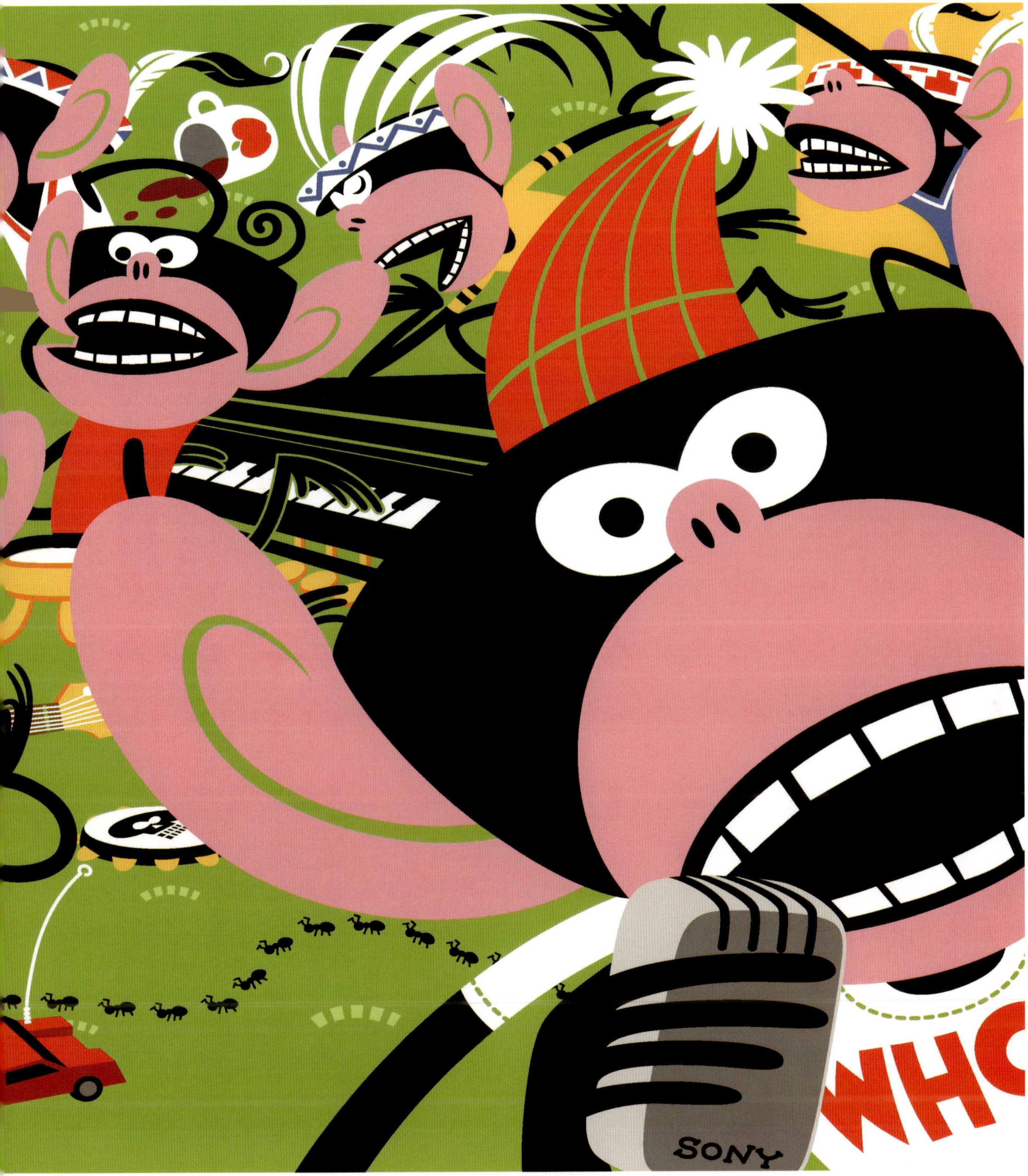
SONY

TITLE : Momo's Wondful Travel
ARTIST : Wu Yanbing
COUNTRY : China
MEDIUM : Vector [Computer Graphics]

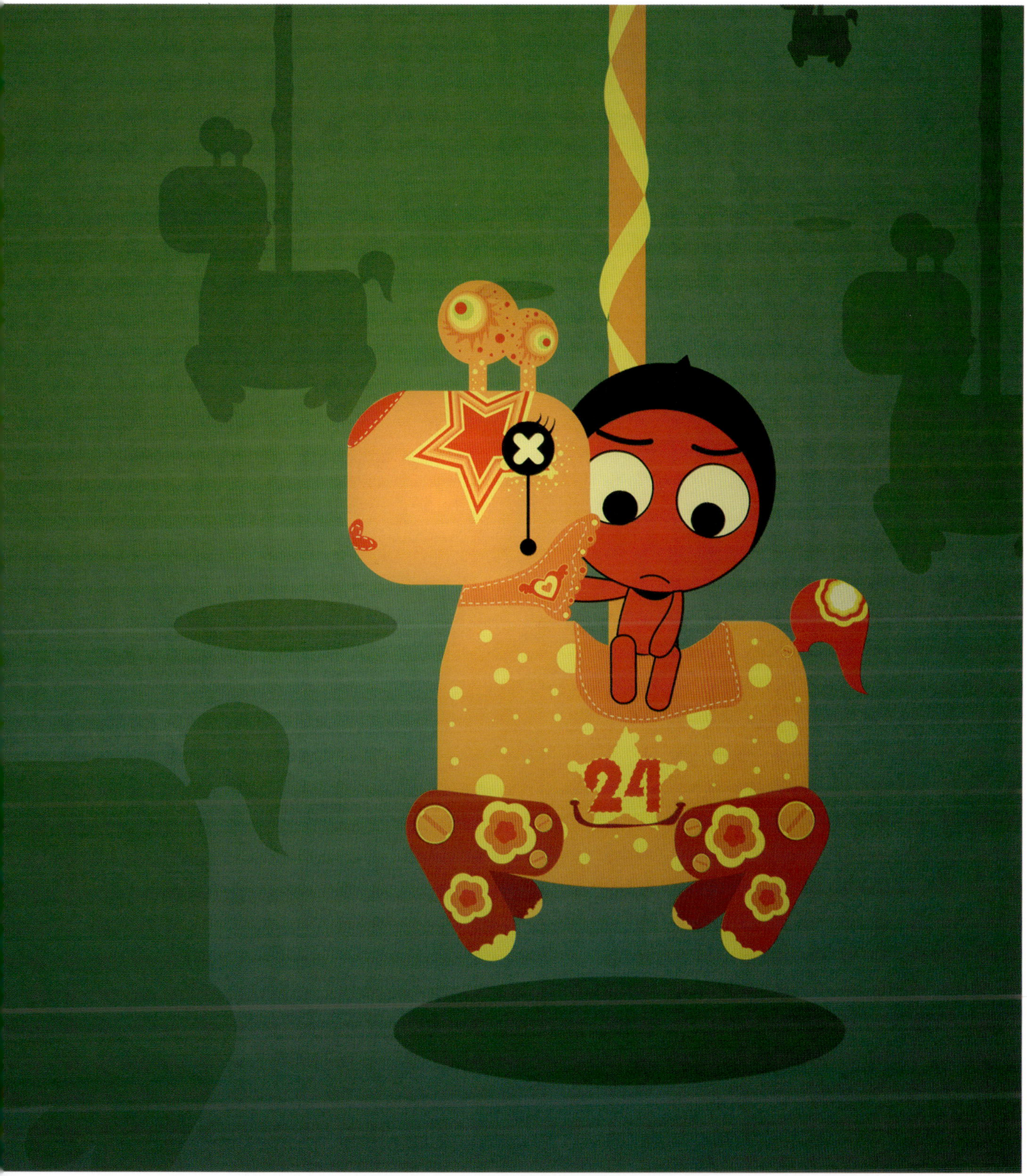
24

TITLE : Freak is great
ARTIST : Driv
COUNTRY : Malaysia
MEDIUM : Vector [Computer Graphics]

127

TITLE : Hero
ARTIST : Driv
COUNTRY : Malaysia
MEDIUM : Vector [Computer Graphics]

TITLE : Autumn
ARTIST : A Moxilin
COUNTRY : China
MEDIUM : Vector [Computer Graphics]

TITLE : My own world
ARTIST : A Moxilin
COUNTRY : China
MEDIUM : Vector [Computer Graphics]

TITLE : Ride Ther Ockett
ARTIST : Paulo Arraiano
COUNTRY : UK
MEDIUM : Vector [Computer Graphics]

TITLE : Brand characters
ARTIST : Shiraz Fuman
COUNTRY : Israel
MEDIUM : Vector [Computer Graphics]

131

132

TITLE : Identikit
ARTIST : Gustavo Torres & Clara Luzian
COUNTRY : Argentina
MEDIUM : Vector [Computer Graphics]

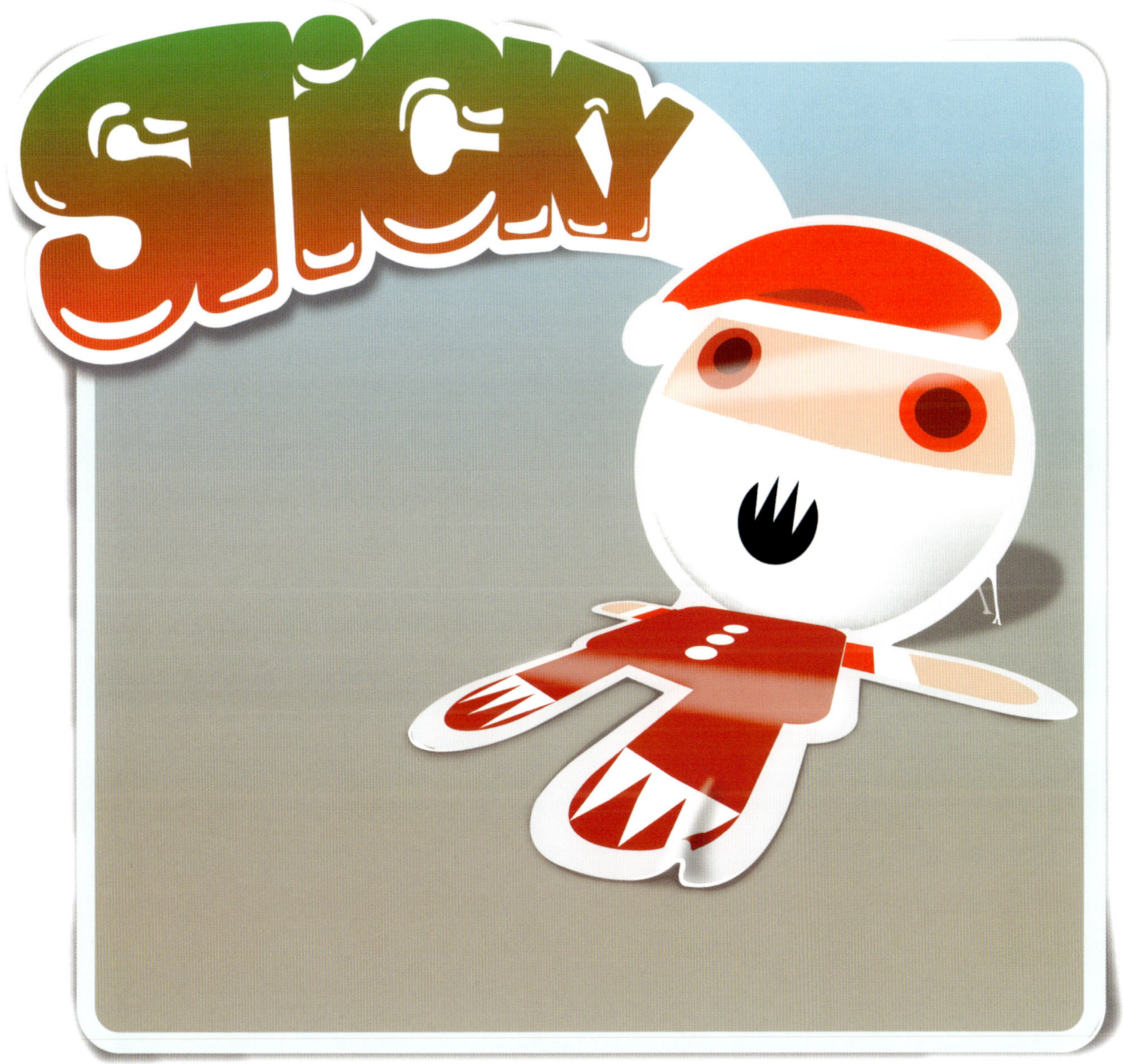
STICKY

134

TITLE : Songsong
ARTIST : Song Han
COUNTRY : China
MEDIUM : Vector [Computer Graphics]

TITLE : Injured trees
ARTIST : Song Han
COUNTRY : China
MEDIUM : Vector [Computer Graphics]

136

This is Songsong's showtime

TITLE : Songsong
ARTIST : Song Han
COUNTRY : China
MEDIUM : Vector [Computer Graphics]

TITLE : Songsong
ARTIST : Song Han
COUNTRY : China
MEDIUM : Vector [Computer Graphics]

138

TITLE : Demon
ARTIST : Song Han
COUNTRY : China
MEDIUM : Vector [Computer Graphics]

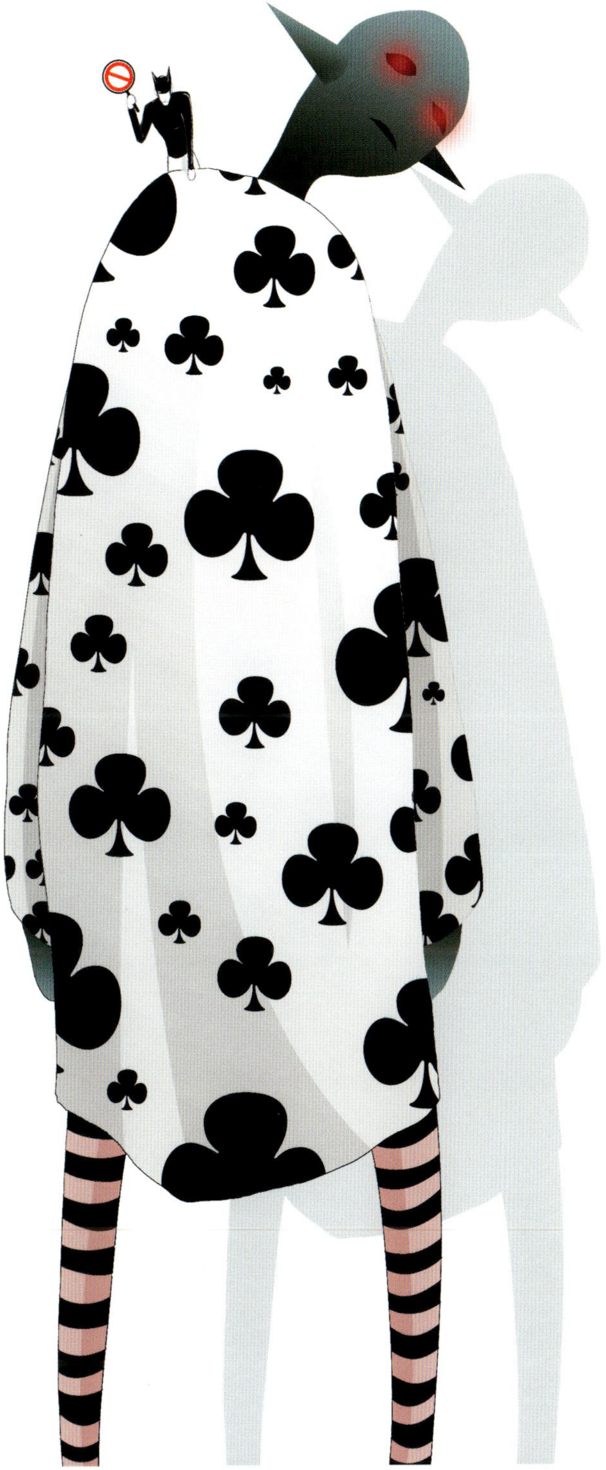

140

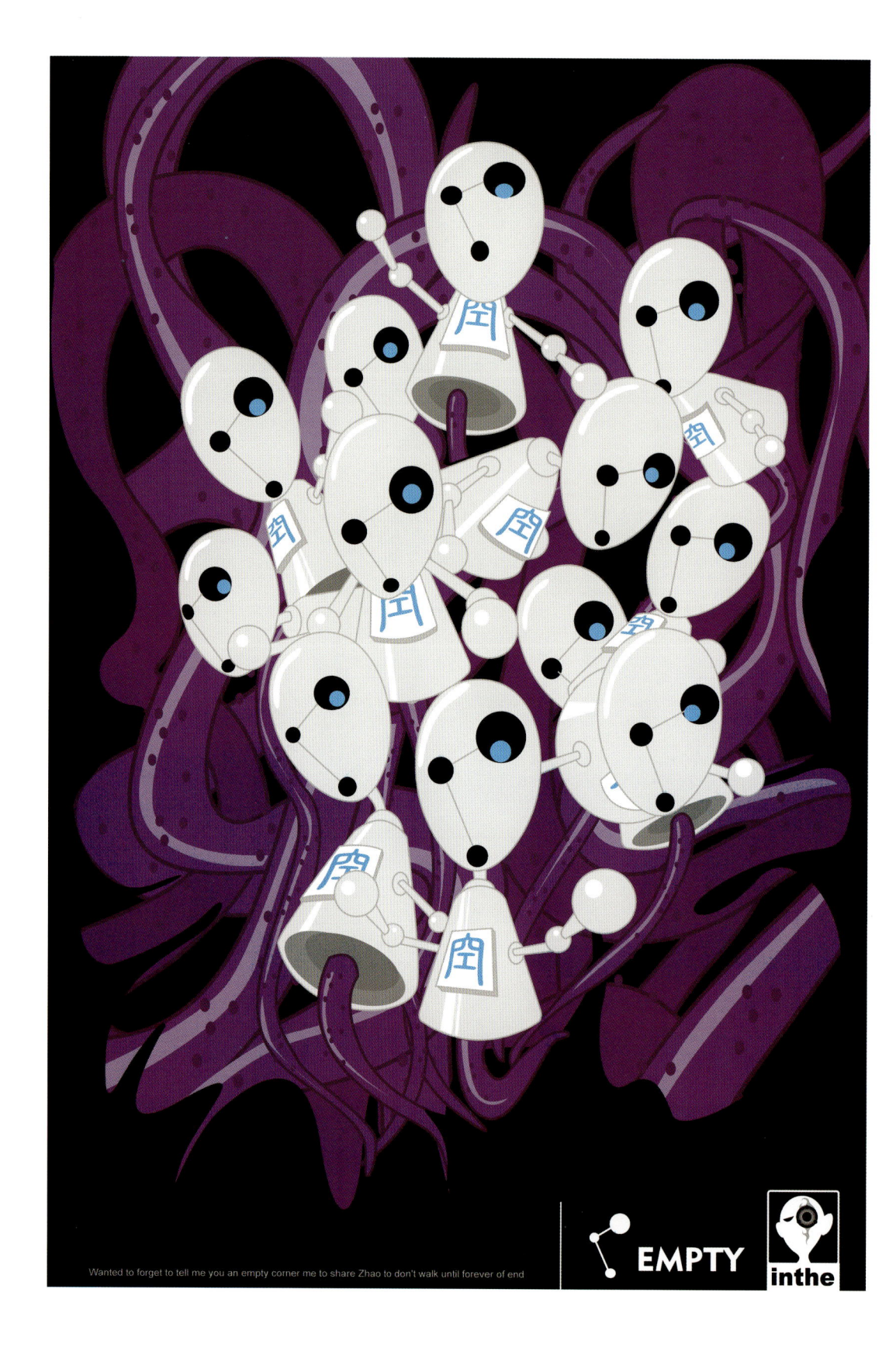

Wanted to forget to tell me you an empty corner me to share Zhao to don't walk until forever of end

EMPTY
inthe

TITLE : Empty
ARTIST : Feng Jie
COUNTRY : China
MEDIUM : Vector [Computer Graphics]

hunger

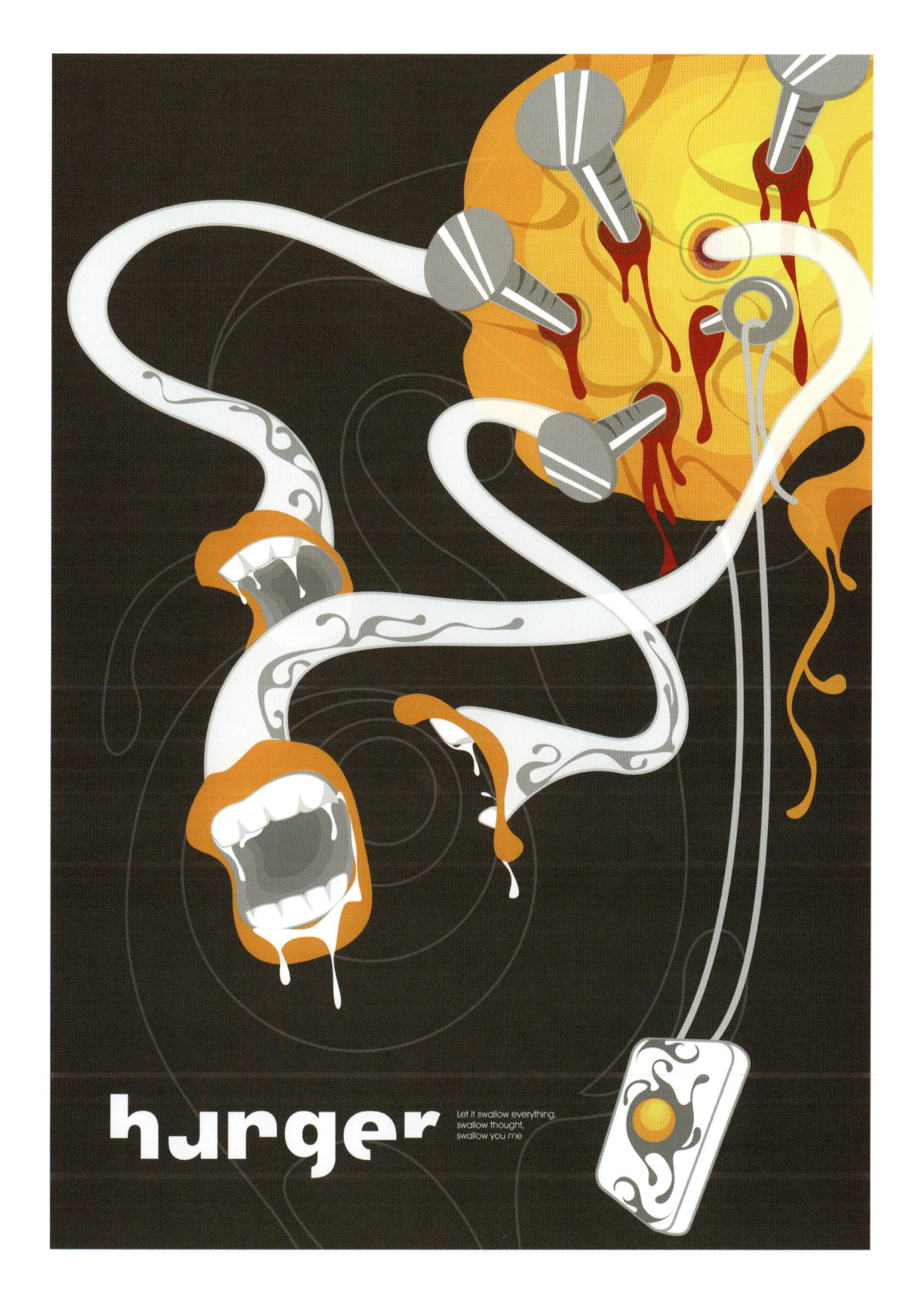

Let it swallow everything,
swallow thought,
swallow you me

142

TITLE : Tongminghua
ARTIST : Li Jinru
COUNTRY : China
MEDIUM : Vector [Computer Graphics]

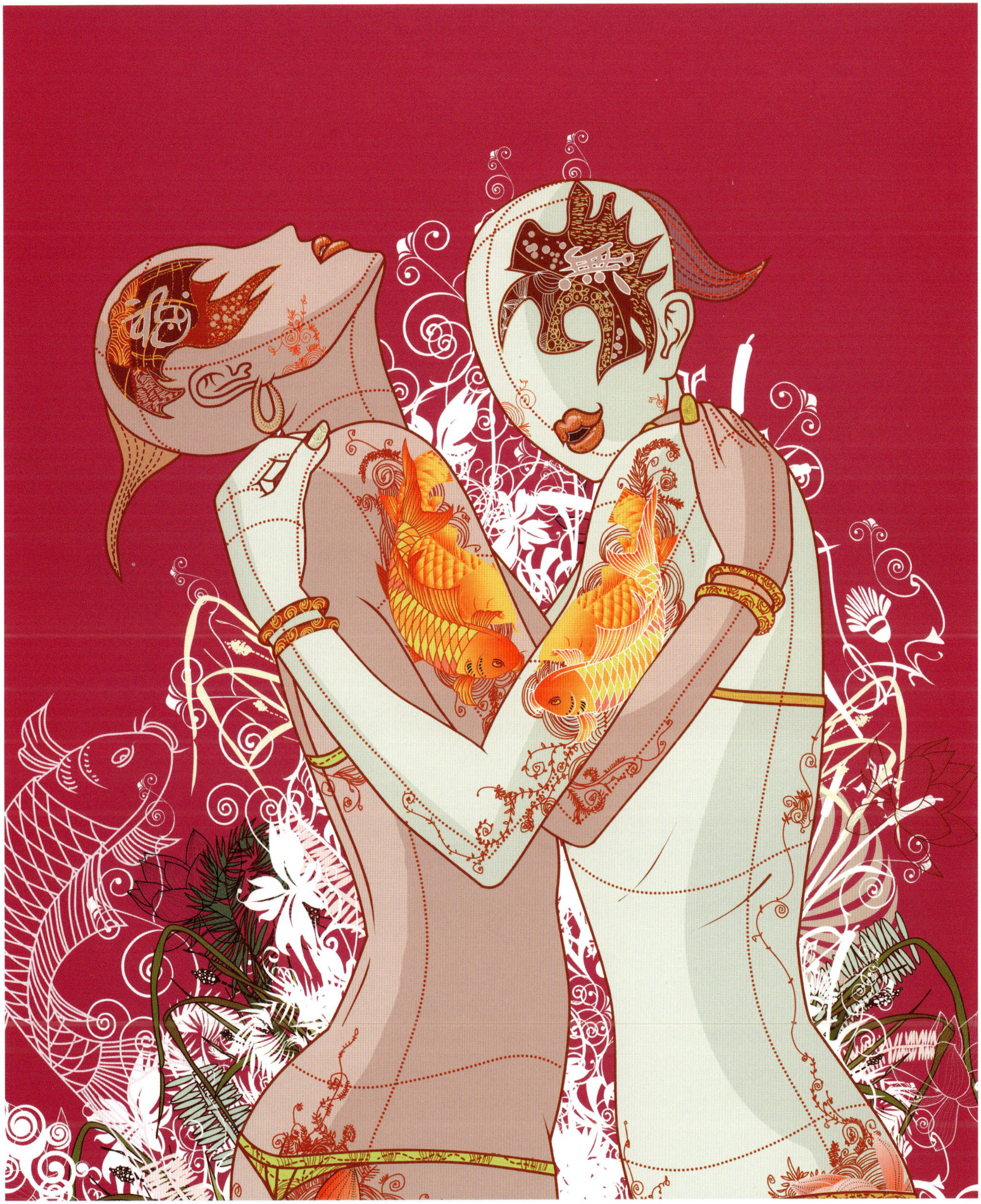

TITLE : Religion Baby
ARTIST : Li Jinru
COUNTRY : China
MEDIUM : Vector [Computer Graphics]

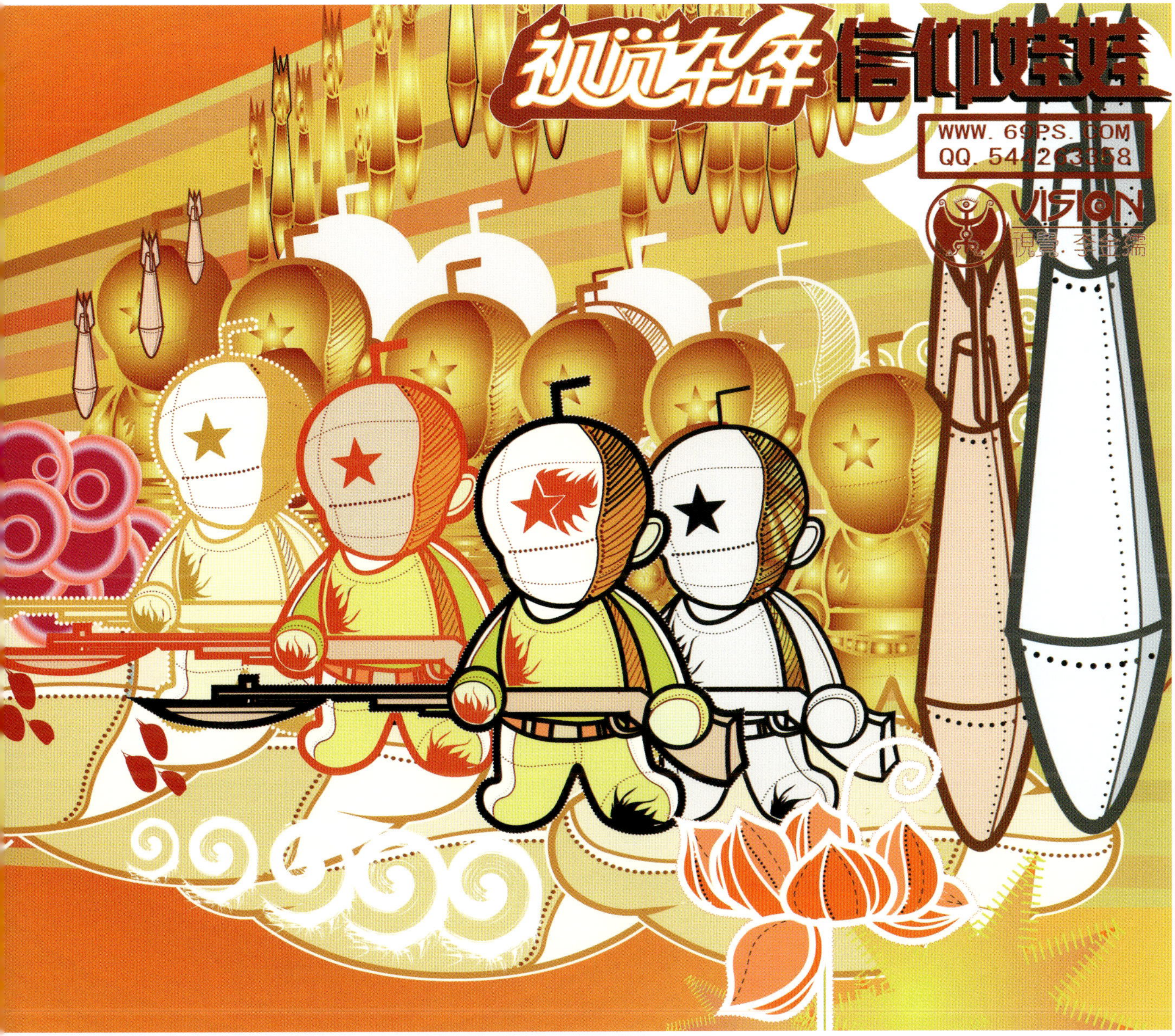
视觉杂碎
信仰娃娃
WWW. 69PS. COM
QQ. 544263358
VISION
視覺. 李金

TITLE : Cbern
ARTIST : Cutting Edge Design Studio
COUNTRY : US
MEDIUM : Vector [Computer Graphics]

TITLE : Door
ARTIST : Lin Xupan
COUNTRY : China
MEDIUM : Vector [Computer Graphics]

148

MADING

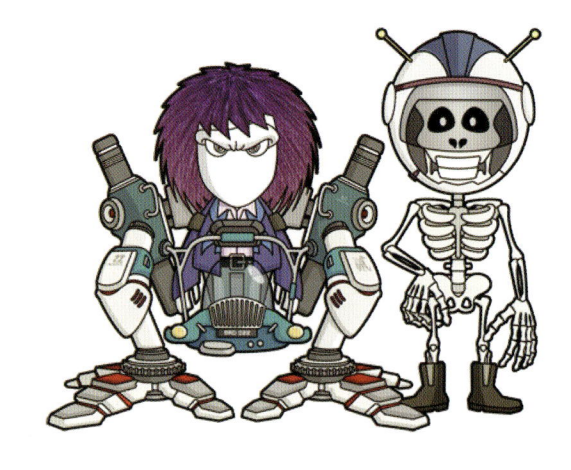

LUDEJIN

TITLE : Woodylailail
ARTIST : Liangliang LIU
COUNTRY : China
MEDIUM : Vector [Computer Graphics]

WoodyLAILAI
WWW.ULABABA.COM
N'EMPLOIE PAS TROP DE LANGUES
NOUVEAUX DÉBUTS D'ICI À ÉDITER
I ET TOUT LE MONDE SONT MÊME, PRÉVOIT LE NOUVEAU SPLENDOR

149

All other product, font and company names and logos are trademarks or registered trademarks of their respective companies.

150

TITLE : AMMUNITION-A
ARTIST : Feng Jie
COUNTRY : China
MEDIUM : Vector [Computer Graphics]

TITLE : AMMUNITION-A
ARTIST : Feng Jie
COUNTRY : China
MEDIUM : Vector [Computer Graphics]

152

TITLE : Time boy
ARTIST : Xu Bing
COUNTRY : China
MEDIUM : Vector [Computer Graphics]

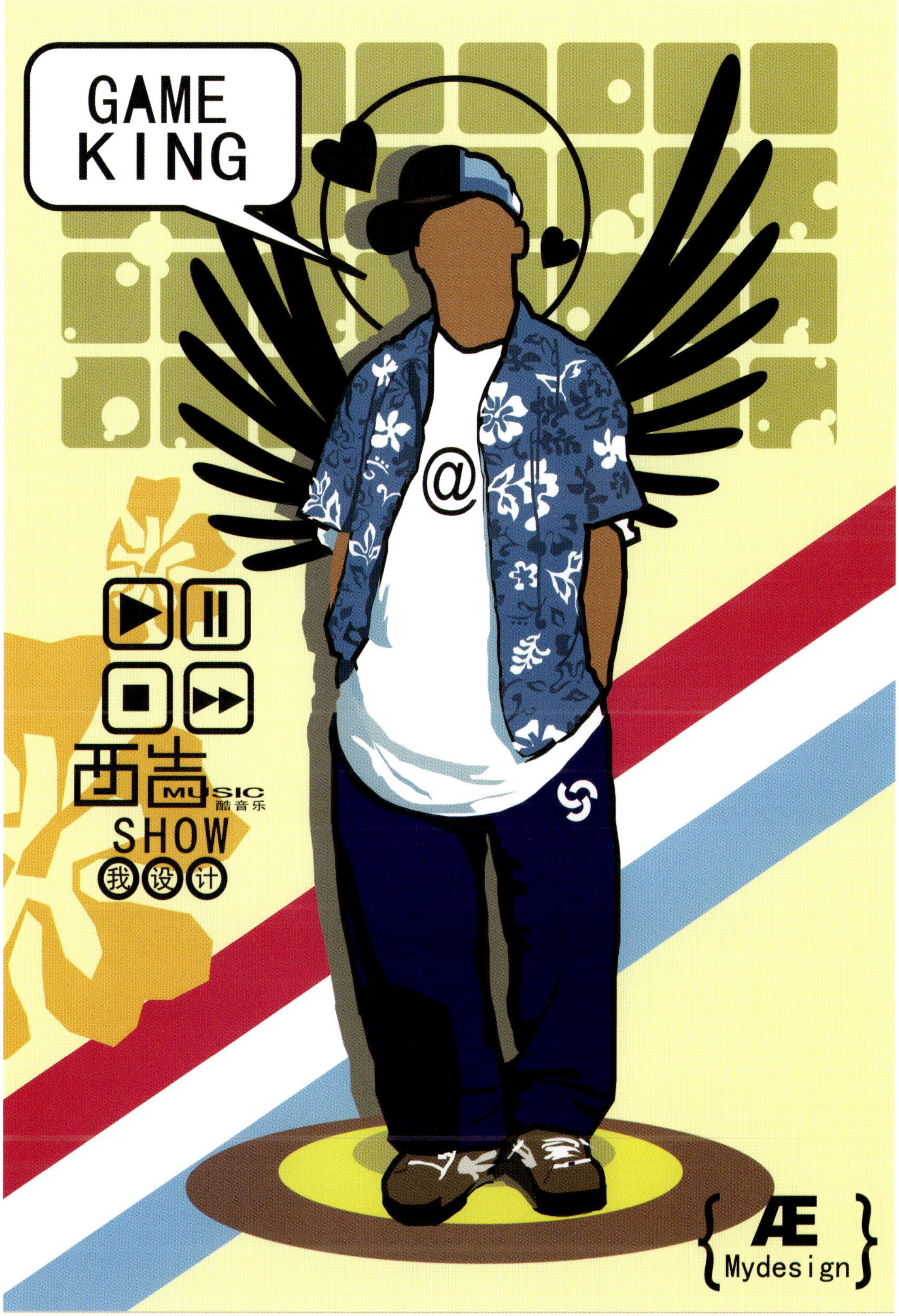
GAME
KING
MUSIC
酷音乐
SHOW
我设计
Æ
Mydesign

TITLE : Fantastic World
ARTIST : Lin Xupan
COUNTRY : China
MEDIUM : Vector [Computer Graphics]

155

TITLE : Roborobo
ARTIST : Driv
COUNTRY : Malaysia
MEDIUM : Vector [Computer Graphics]

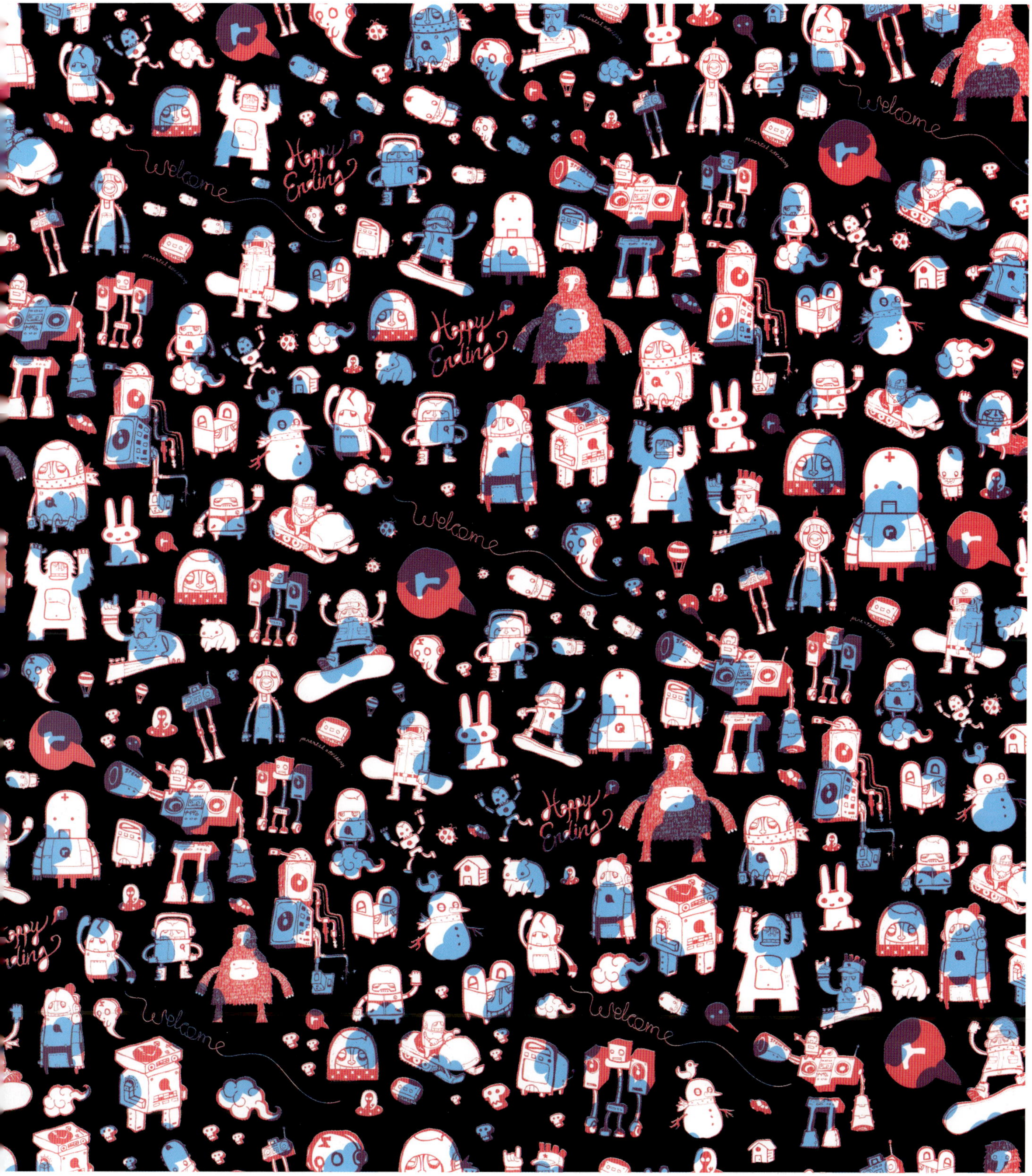
Welcome
Happy Ending

158

Honda CIVIC

TITLE : Yu Linjun
ARTIST : Wang Peng
COUNTRY : China
MEDIUM : Vector [Computer Graphics]

TITLE : Happy Spring Festival
ARTIST : Wang Peng
COUNTRY : China
MEDIUM : Vector [Computer Graphics]

TITLE : Outer Space
ARTIST : Miwo
COUNTRY : China
MEDIUM : Vector [Computer Graphics]

TITLE : Happy journey
ARTIST : Miwo
COUNTRY : China
MEDIUM : Vector [Computer Graphics]

TITLE : End of chapter 07
ARTIST : Mclelun
COUNTRY : Malaysia
MEDIUM : Vector [Computer Graphics]

END OF CHAPTER 07
ILLUSTRATED BY MCLELUN

TITLE : Mask
ARTIST : Mclelun
COUNTRY : Malaysia
MEDIUM : Vector [Computer Graphics]

TITLE : Help the kid
ARTIST : Mclelun
COUNTRY : Malaysia
MEDIUM : Vector [Computer Graphics]

TITLE : Hairy
ARTIST : Mark Verhaagen
COUNTRY : The Netherlands
MEDIUM : Vector [Computer Graphics]

TITLE : Flyingbots
ARTIST : Mark Verhaagen
COUNTRY : The Netherlands
MEDIUM : Vector [Computer Graphics]

TITLE : Hiding
ARTIST : Mark Verhaagen
COUNTRY : The Netherlands
MEDIUM : Vector [Computer Graphics]

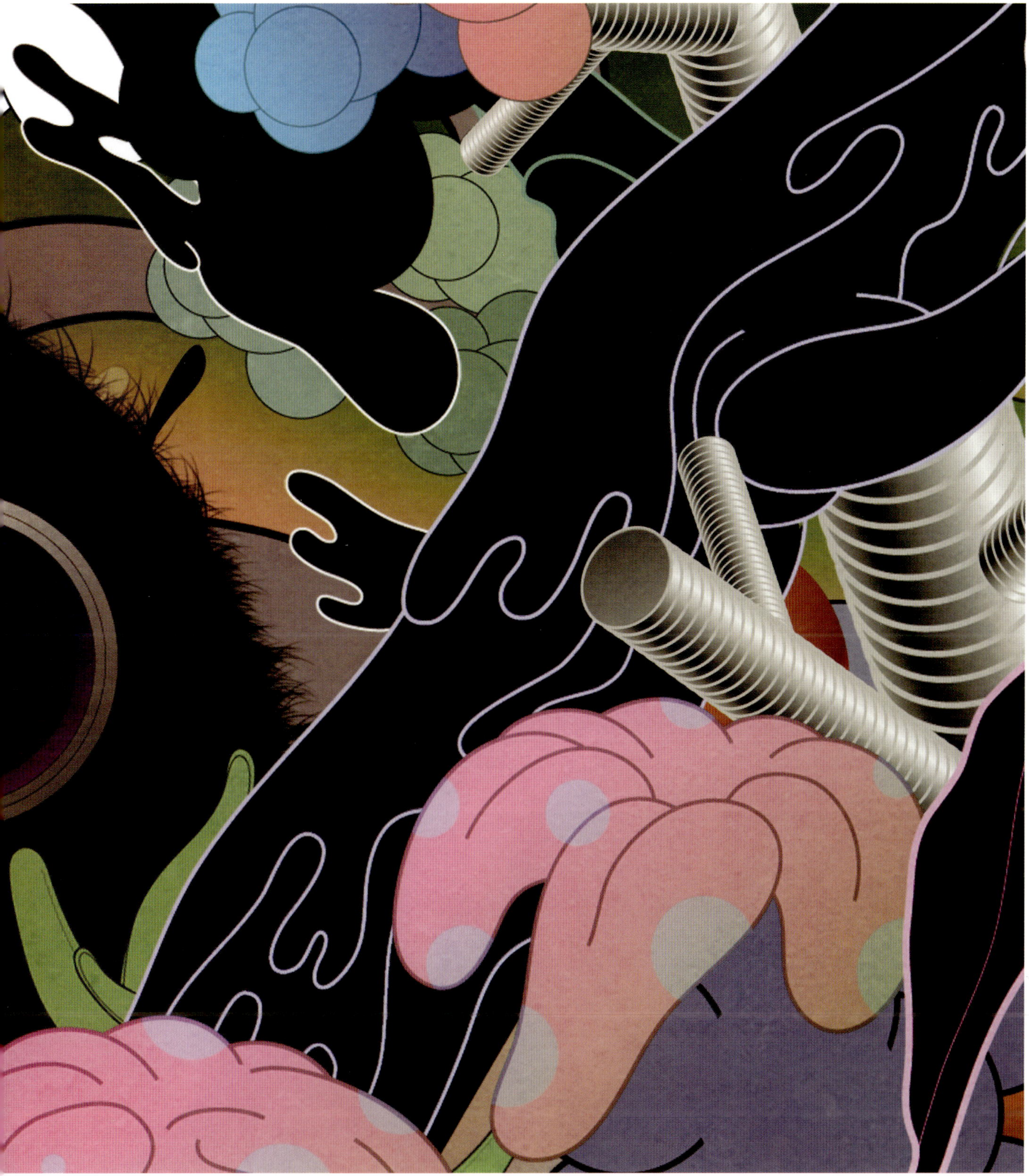

TITLE : Do not disturb me!
ARTIST : Chaos
COUNTRY : China Taiwan
MEDIUM : Computer Painting

TITLE : The Gift from Devil
ARTIST : Chaos
COUNTRY : China Taiwan
MEDIUM : Computer Painting

TITLE : Affection
ARTIST : Lee Zhuoyan
COUNTRY : China
MEDIUM : Vector [Computer Graphics]

173

TITLE : Mr. Fang
ARTIST : Blessing Ear
COUNTRY : China
MEDIUM : Vector [Computer Graphics]

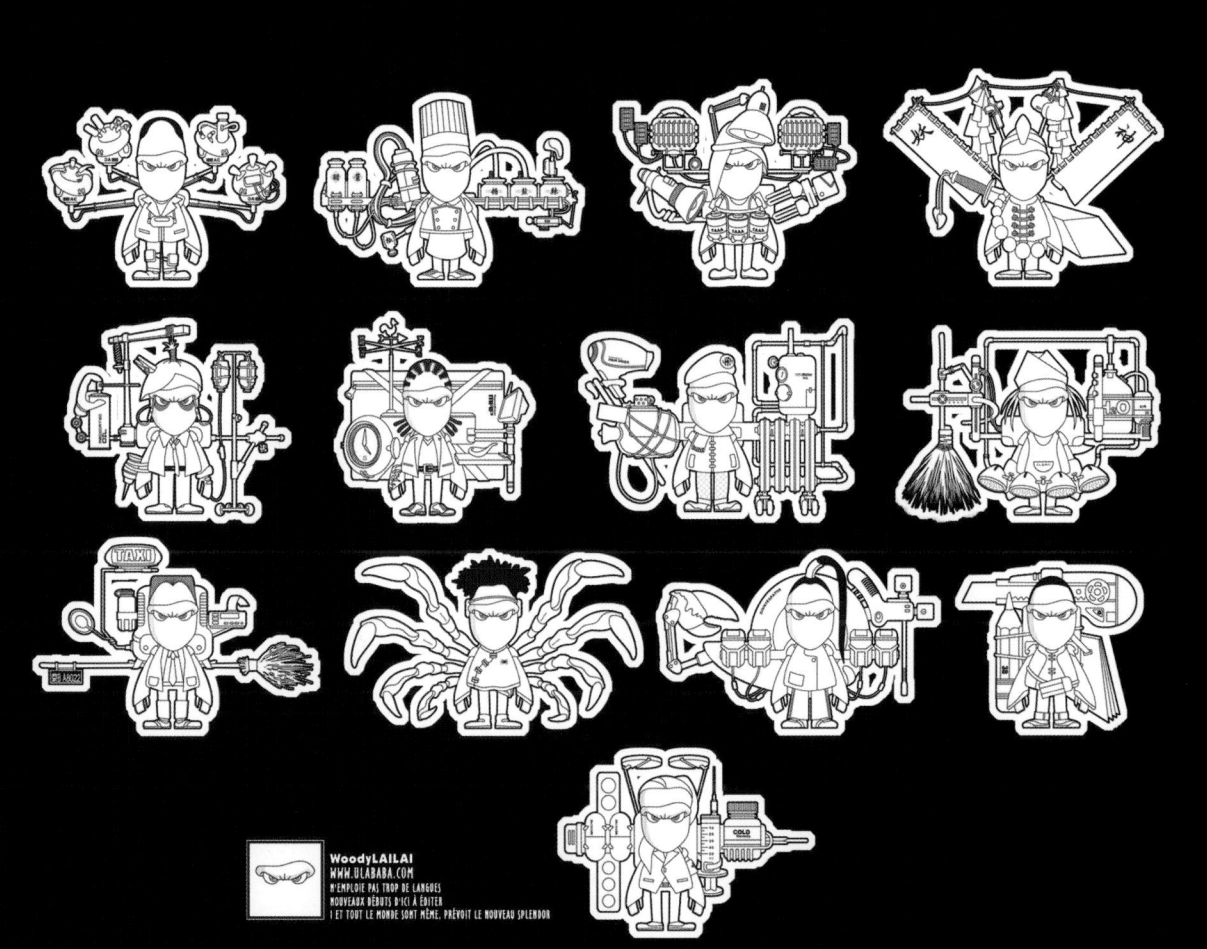

175

TITLE : Woodylailail
ARTIST : Liangliang LIU
COUNTRY : China
MEDIUM : Vector [Computer Graphics]

TITLE : Woodylailail
ARTIST : Liangliang LIU
COUNTRY : China
MEDIUM : Vector [Computer Graphics]

177

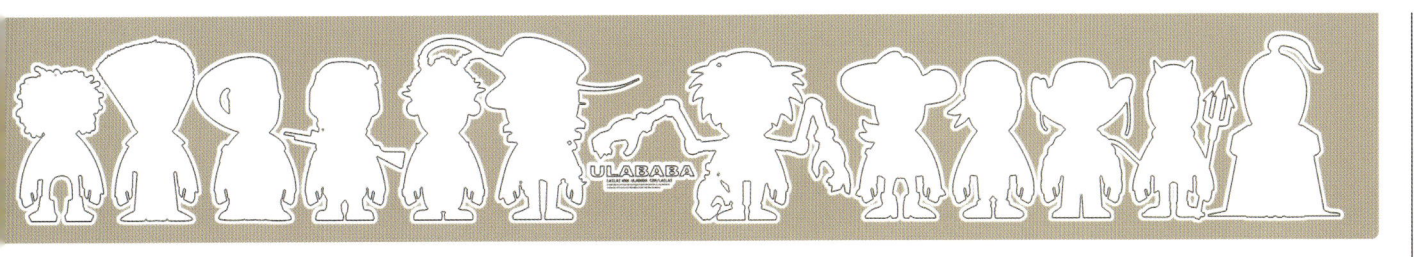

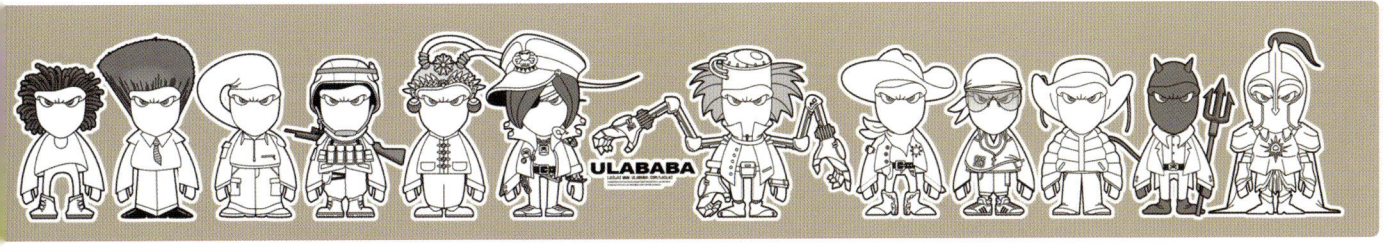

TITLE : Characteristic Icon
ARTIST : Undoboy
COUNTRY : US
MEDIUM : Vector [Computer Graphics]

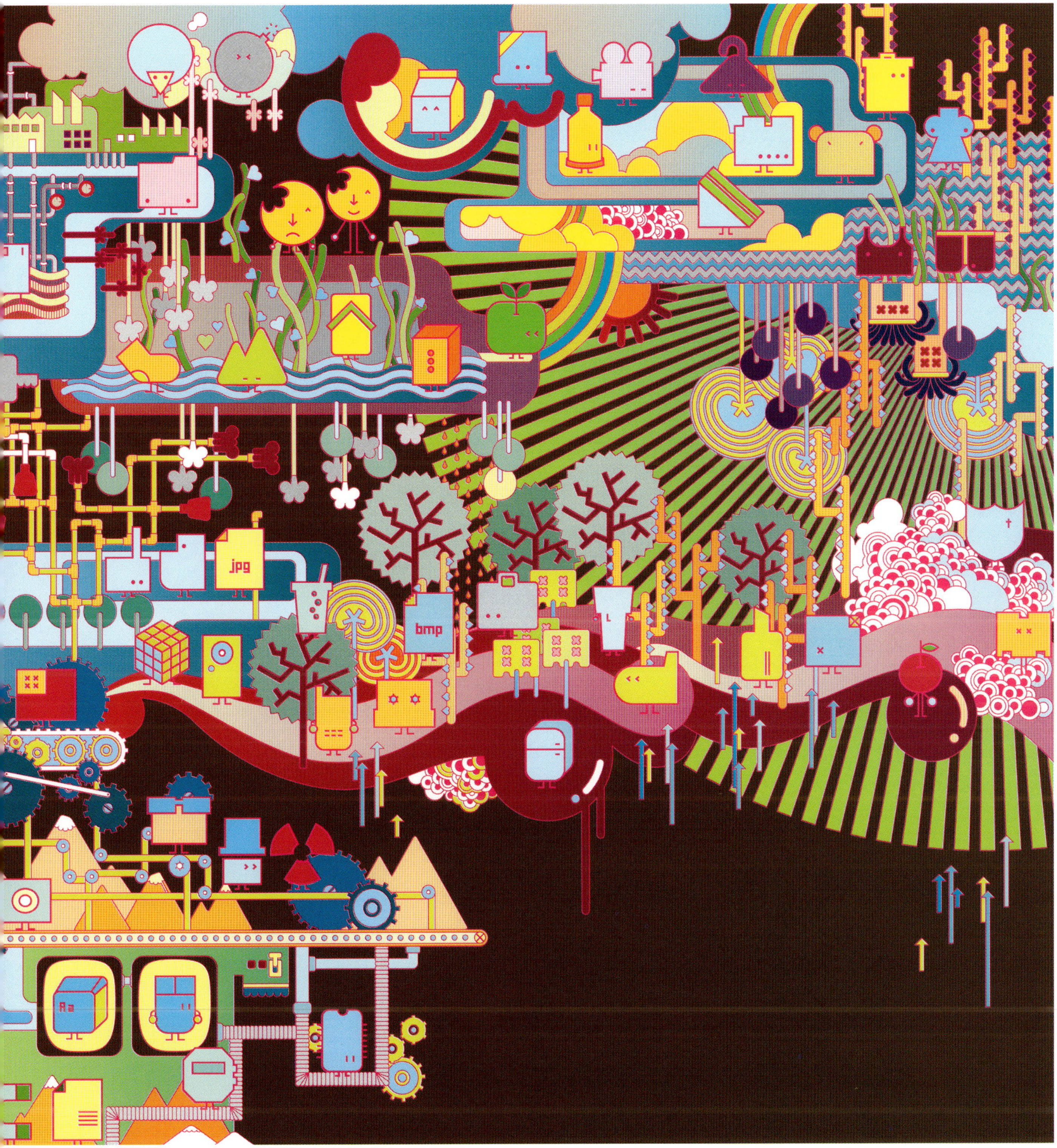
jpg
bmp

TITLE : Kurumach
ARTIST : Haruki Higashi
COUNTRY : Japan
MEDIUM : Vector [Computer Graphics]

TITLE : Sstv
ARTIST : Haruki Higashi
COUNTRY : Japan
MEDIUM : Vector [Computer Graphics]

182

TITLE : Typolowgies
ARTIST : Haruki Higashi
COUNTRY : Japan
MEDIUM : Vector [Computer Graphics]

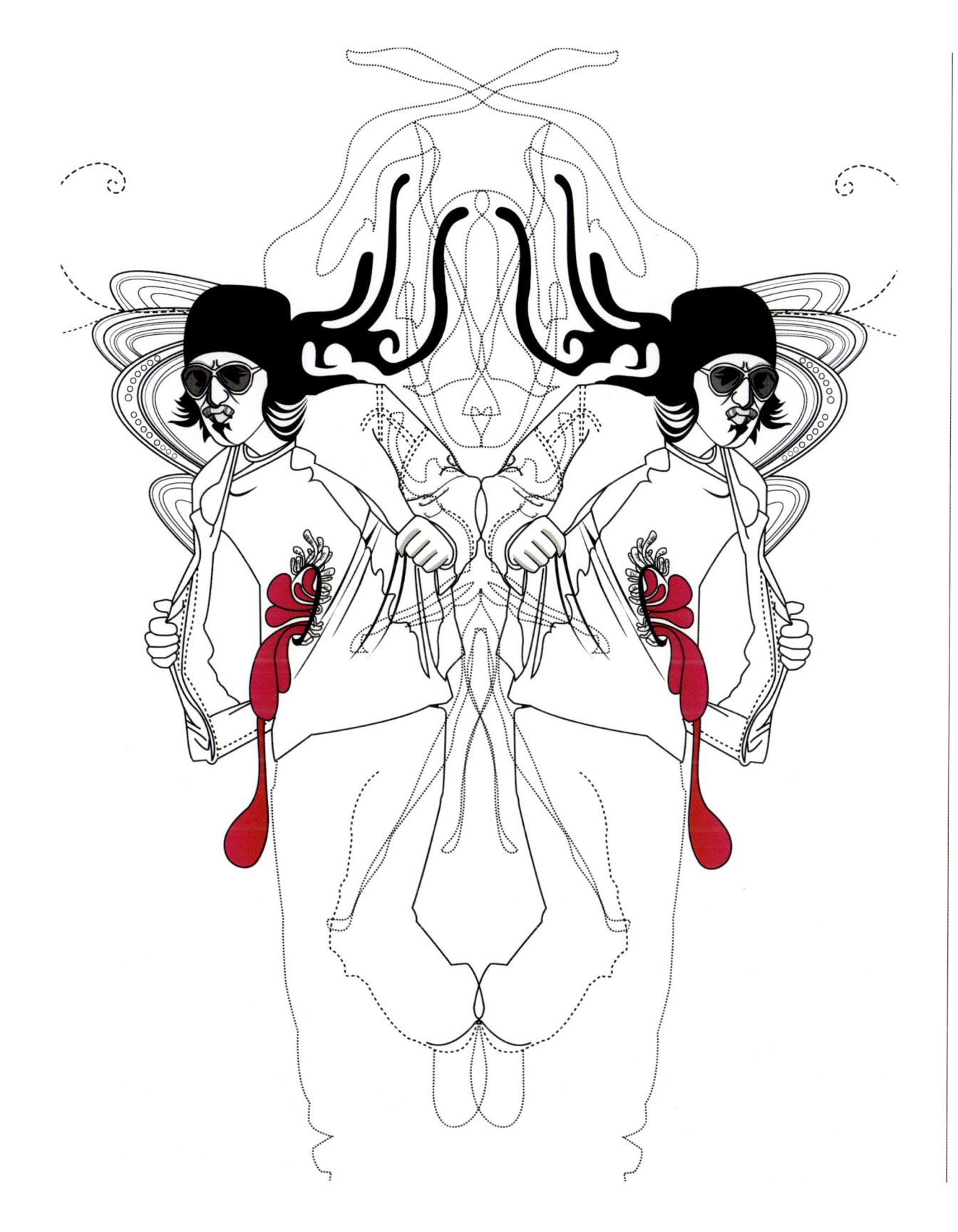

TITLE : Similarities and difference
ARTIST : Miwo
COUNTRY : China
MEDIUM : Vector [Computer Graphics]

TITLE : My baby
ARTIST : Giovanni Paletta
COUNTRY : Italy
MEDIUM : Vector [Computer Graphics]

TITLE : Need for speed
ARTIST : Giovanni Paletta
COUNTRY : Italy
MEDIUM : Vector [Computer Graphics]

Mixed media and collage

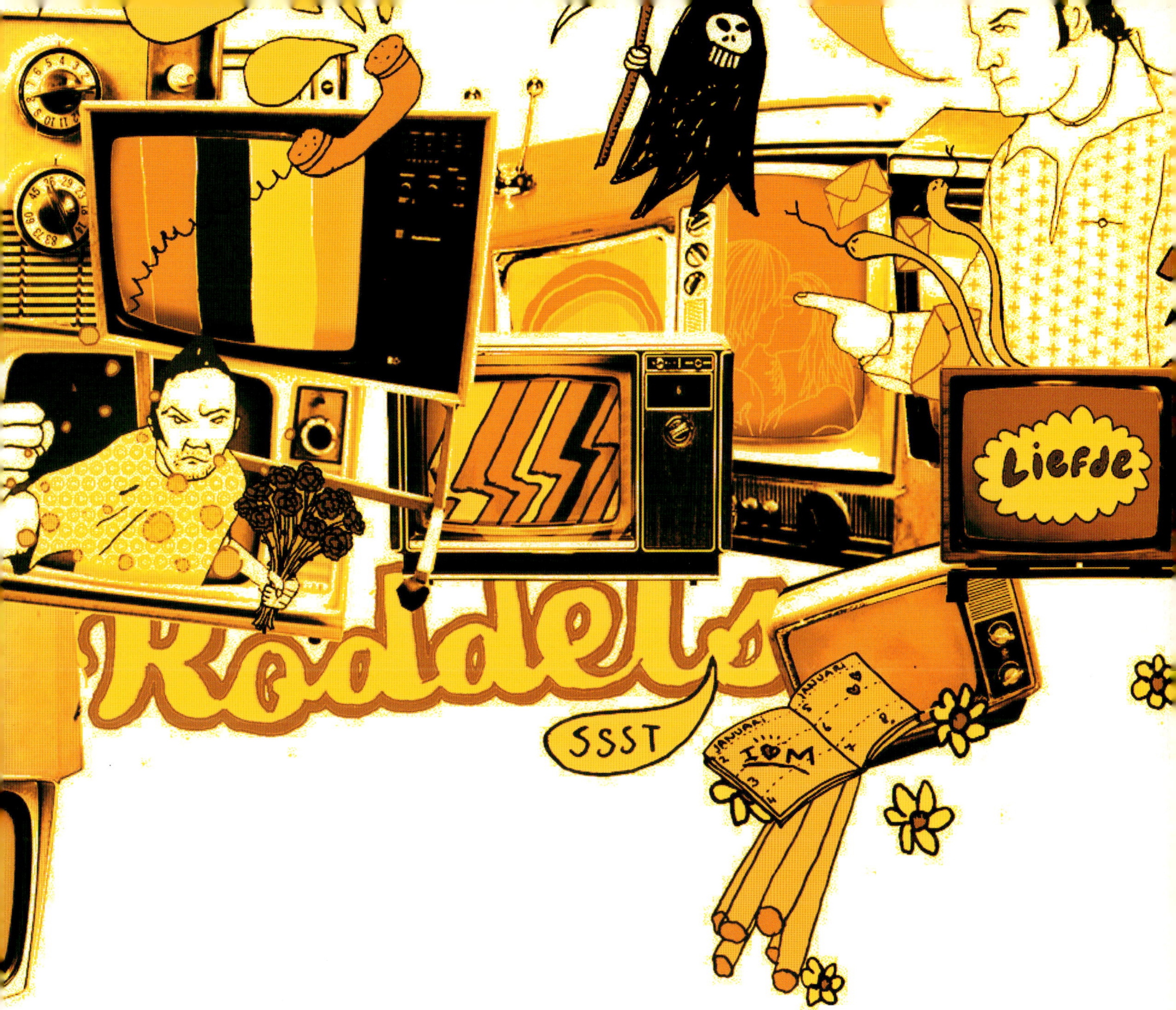

Liefde
Roddels
SSST
Januari
I ♥ M

TITLE : Typewriter x 1
ARTIST : Postgal.com
COUNTRY : China Hongong
MEDIUM : Mixed Media

THE TIRED CITY

TITLE : Halloween Returns
ARTIST : Michael Foster
COUNTRY : US
MEDIUM : Ink Drawing & Vector Rendering

TITLE: Happiness is at your fingertips
ARTIST: Michael Foster
COUNTRY: US
MEDIUM: Ink Drawing & Vector Rendering

TITLE : Thinking
ARTIST : Michael Foster
COUNTRY : US
MEDIUM : Ink Drawing & Vector Rendering

TITLE : Pod People
ARTIST : Michael Foster
COUNTRY : US
MEDIUM : Ink Drawing & Vector Rendering

TITLE : Image
ARTIST : Marie-Chantale Turgeon
COUNTRY : Canada
MEDIUM : Pen and Ink, Watercolor and Gouache, Acylic and Oil, Mixed Media and Collage

TITLE : Living out loud
ARTIST : Marie-Chantale Turgeon
COUNTRY : Canada
MEDIUM : Pen and Ink, Watercolor and Gouache, Acylic and Oil, Mixed Media and Collage

TITLE : Traveling Dreamer in Japan
ARTIST : Marie-Chantale Turgeon
COUNTRY : Canada
MEDIUM : Pen and Ink, Watercolor and Gouache, Mixed Media and Collage

TITLE : Traveling Dreamer
ARTIST : Marie-Chantale Turgeon
COUNTRY : Canada
MEDIUM : Pen and Ink, Watercolor and Gouache, Mixed Media and Collage

TITLE : King of convenience, i'd rather dance
ARTIST : Marie-Chantale Turgeon
COUNTRY : Canada
MEDIUM : Pen and Ink, Acylic and Oil, Mixed Media and Collage

I'd rather dance than talk with you

TITLE : Couple
ARTIST : Yuhoo
COUNTRY : China
MEDIUM : Pen and Ink, Acylic and Oil, Mixed Media and Collage

TITLE : Lina Fox
ARTIST : Yuhoo
COUNTRY : China
MEDIUM : Pen and Ink, Acylic and Oil, Mixed Media

202

TITLE : Promise tree
ARTIST : Yuhoo
COUNTRY : China
MEDIUM : Pen and Ink, Acylic and Oil, Mixed Media

TITLE : Lattice umbrella after midnight
ARTIST : Yuhoo
COUNTRY : China
MEDIUM : Pen and Ink, Acylic and Oil, Mixed Media

TITLE : Eden
ARTIST : Yu Lin
COUNTRY : China
MEDIUM : Mixed Media

205

TITLE : Tiedan's xx life
ARTIST : Shi Wuxuan
COUNTRY : China
MEDIUM : Pen and Ink, Pencil, Mixed Media and Collage

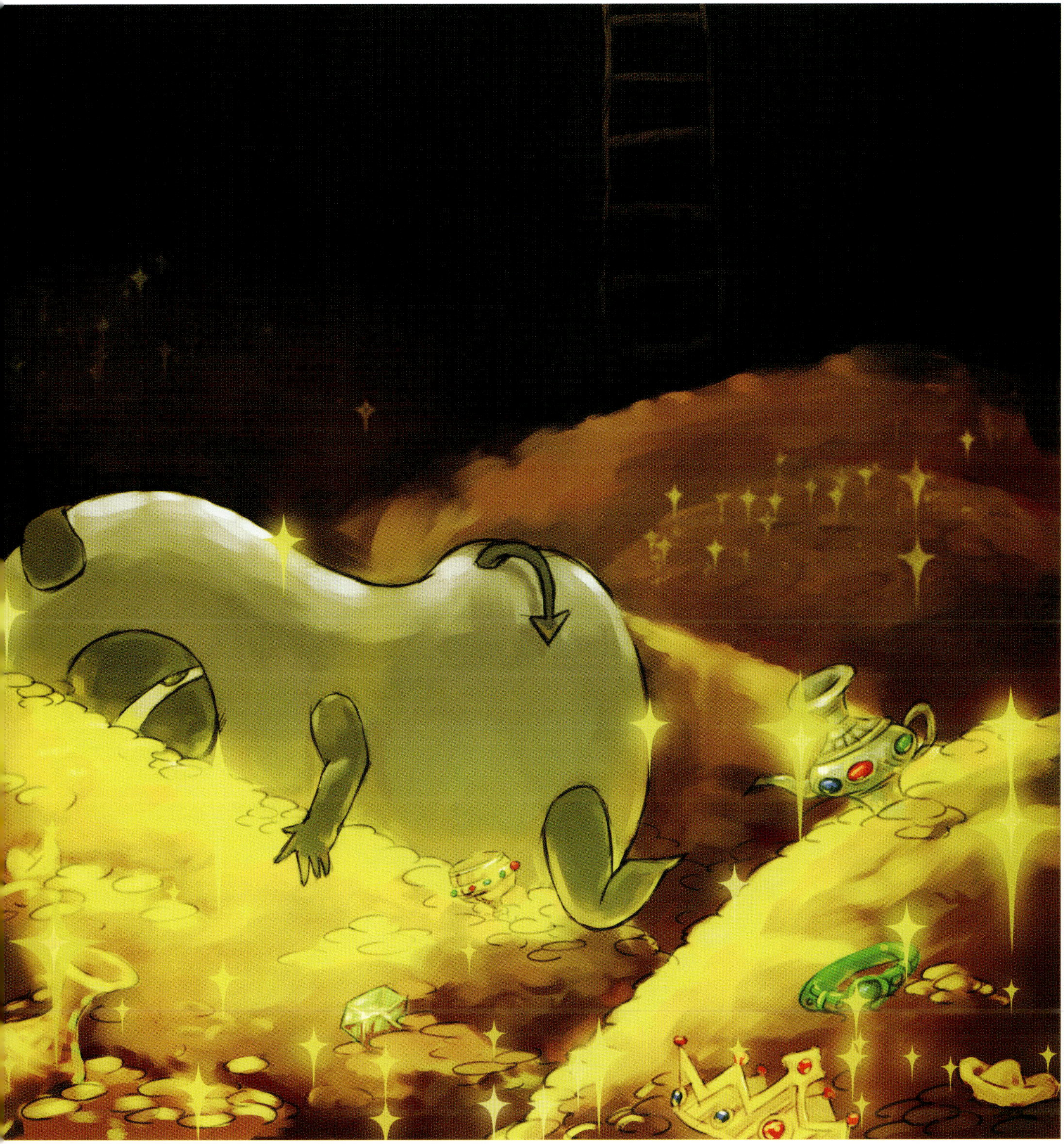

TITLE : Little Friend
ARTIST : Yu Lin
COUNTRY : China
MEDIUM : Mixed Media and Collage

TITLE : The Lost Necklace
ARTIST : Yu Lin
COUNTRY : China
MEDIUM : Mixed Media and Collage

TITLE: Expectation
ARTIST: Shi Wuxuan
COUNTRY: China
MEDIUM: Pen and Ink, Pencil, Mixed Media and Collage

把自己种在土里，能长出什么来？

TITLE : I won't let you know!
ARTIST : Shi Wuxuan
COUNTRY : China
MEDIUM : Pen and Ink, Pencil, Mixed Media and Collage

212

TITLE : Stark-naked Angel
ARTIST : Goldfish
COUNTRY : China
MEDIUM : Mixed Media and Collage

213

TITLE : Valentine's Day
ARTIST : Heng Lan
COUNTRY : China
MEDIUM : Mixed media

TITLE : Face-painting Room
ARTIST : Heng Lan
COUNTRY : China
MEDIUM : Mixed media

215

TITLE : Restless
ARTIST : Goldfish
COUNTRY : China
MEDIUM : Mixed Media and Collage

TITLE : Snowman
ARTIST : Goldfish
COUNTRY : China
MEDIUM : Mixed Media and Collage

TITLE : Misheard Lyrics, Nme Magazine
ARTIST : Serge Seidlitz
COUNTRY : UK
MEDIUM : Pen and Ink, Pencil, Vector [Computer Graphics]

TITLE : Teen Wolf
ARTIST : Serge Seidlitz
COUNTRY : UK
MEDIUM : Pen and Ink, Pencil, Vector [Computer Graphics]

TITLE : Survival Kit
ARTIST : Serge Seidlitz
COUNTRY : UK
MEDIUM : Pen and Ink, Pencil, Vector [Computer Graphics]

IN GOOD COMPANY

TITLE : 35th anniversary of adidas
ARTIST : Wang Peng
COUNTRY : China
MEDIUM : Pen and Ink, Pencil, Vector [Computer Graphics]

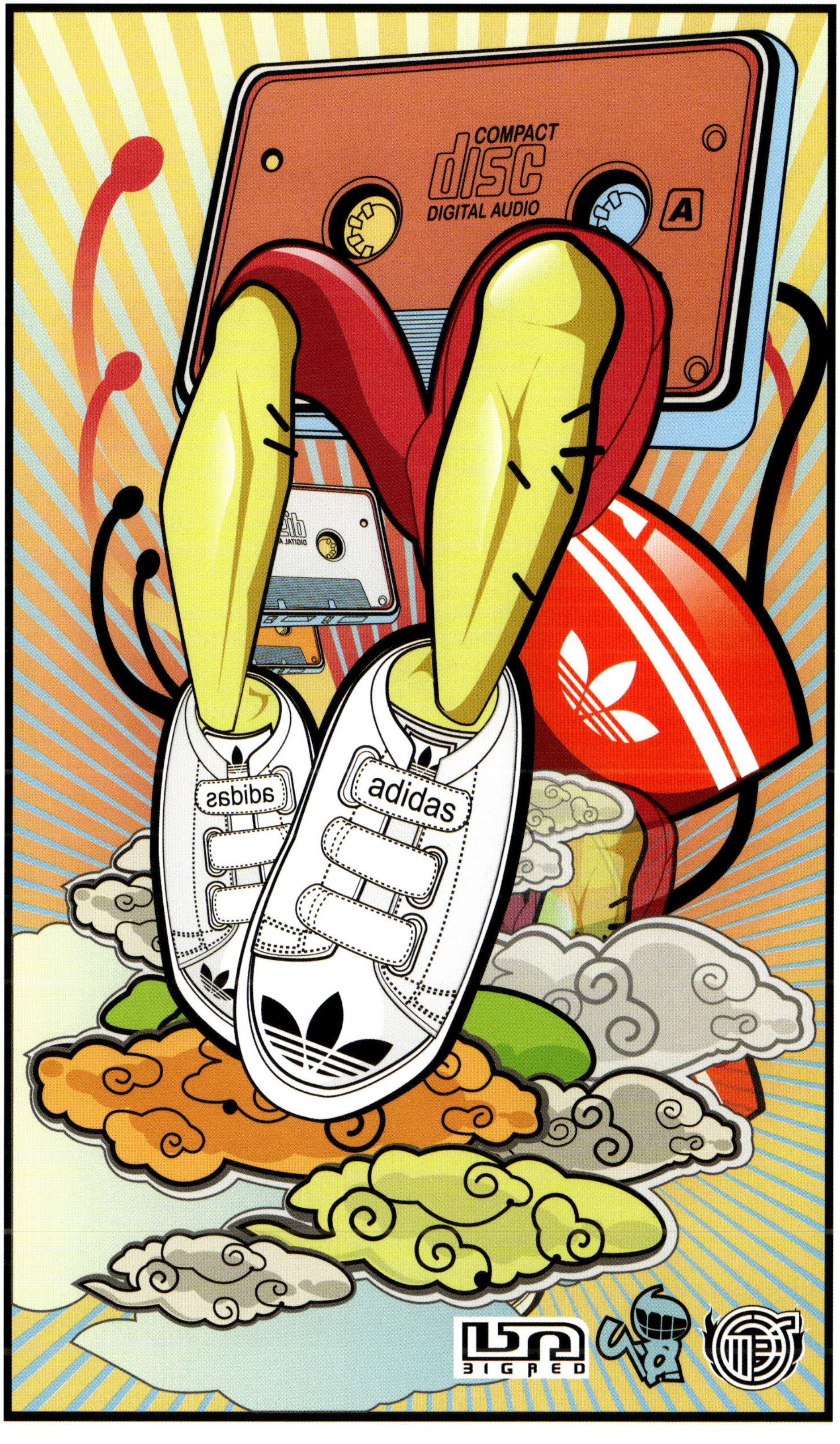
COMPACT
disc
DIGITAL AUDIO
A
adidas
adidas
BIGRED

TITLE : Cabaret Festival
ARTIST : MAKI
COUNTRY : The Netherlands
MEDIUM : Mixed media | Photoshop

TITLE : Camping [Wallet Design]
ARTIST : MAKI
COUNTRY : The Netherlands
MEDIUM : Mixed media | Photoshop

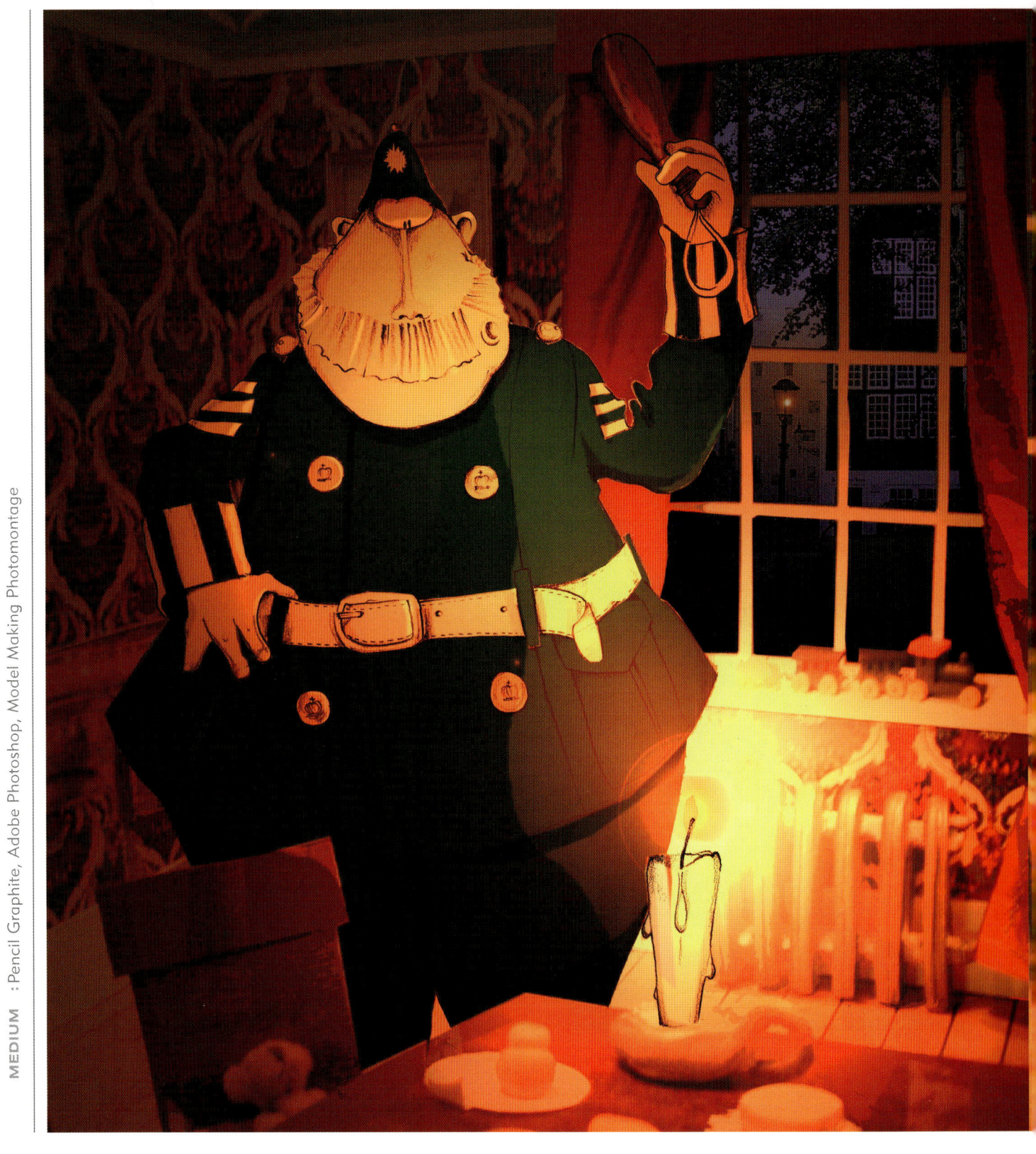

TITLE : Blow Candle
ARTIST : Steve Stone
COUNTRY : UK
MEDIUM : Pencil Graphite, Adobe Photoshop, Model Making Photomontage

pifphuzzer

TITLE : Old Lady
ARTIST : Steve Stone
COUNTRY : UK
MEDIUM : Pencil Photoshop, Model Making, Collage Photo Montage

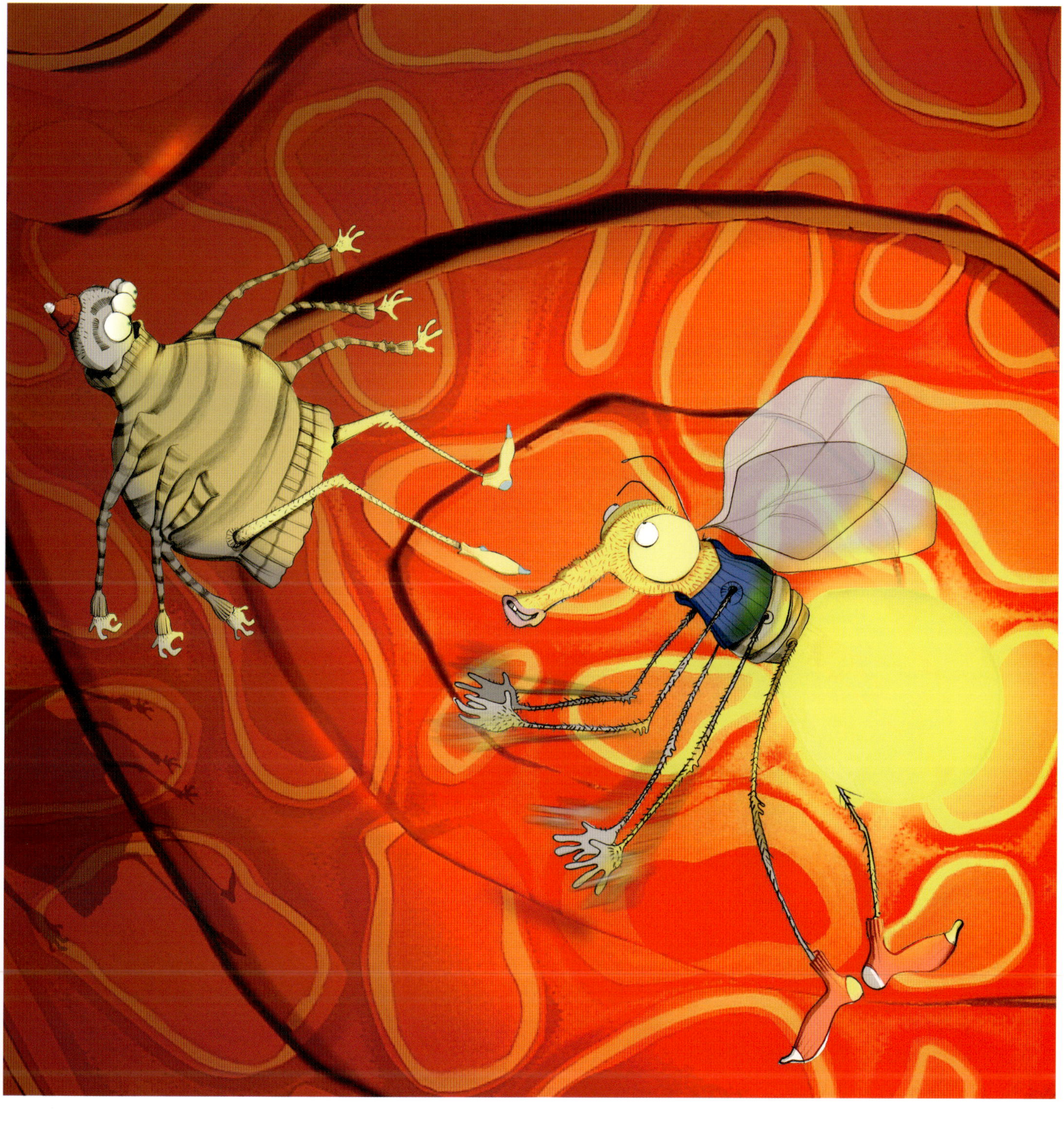

TITLE : I Computer
ARTIST : Lodewyk M. Barkhuizen
COUNTRY : South Africa
MEDIUM : Mixed media | Photoshop

I.HUMAN

I.COMPUTER
FEELING O.K?

i.computer.i.human move mouse. move arm.click!
rotate arm.bend cable.click! see monitor. reflect eye. click!
delete?yes/no

TITLE : Volkswagen Van
ARTIST : MAKI
COUNTRY : The Netherlands
MEDIUM : Mixed media | Photoshop

TITLE : Studenten Band Festival
ARTIST : MAKI
COUNTRY : The Netherlands
MEDIUM : Mixed media | Photoshop

TITLE : Kut & Peest
ARTIST : MAKI
COUNTRY : The Netherlands
MEDIUM : Mixed Media and Collage

TITLE : Musicbox
ARTIST : Paulo Arraiano
COUNTRY : Portugal
MEDIUM : Mixed Media and Collage

TITLE : Brooklyn Summer
ARTIST : Julio Rölle
COUNTRY : Germany
MEDIUM : Mixed Media and Collage

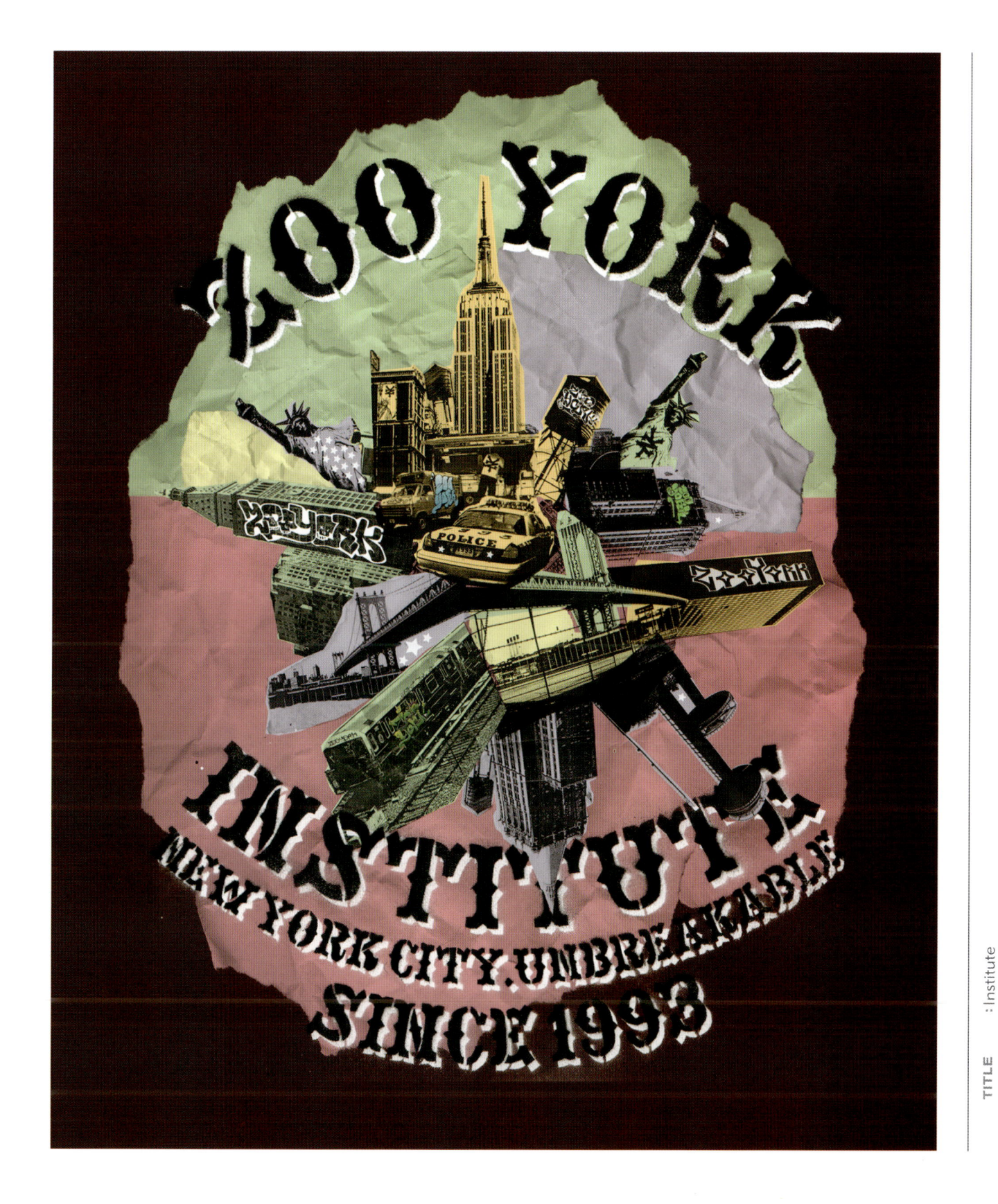

TITLE : Institute
ARTIST : Julio Rölle
COUNTRY : Germany
MEDIUM : Mixed Media and Collage

238

TITLE : Wonderful 2007
ARTIST : Pi Jiupaopao
COUNTRY : China
MEDIUM : Mixed Media and Collage

TITLE : Come! 2007
ARTIST : Pi Jiupaopao
COUNTRY : China
MEDIUM : Mixed Media and Collage

"Follow.Lead? Follow?.Lead.Lead.Lead? Follow!.Lead?"

TITLE : Followlead
ARTIST : Lodewyk M. Barkhuizen
COUNTRY : South Africa
MEDIUM : Mixed Media and Collage

good kid · bad kid

TITLE : Goodkid
ARTIST : Lodewyk M. Barkhuizen
COUNTRY : South Africa
MEDIUM : Mixed Media and Collage

TITLE : Wacky Pig in The Golden Town
ARTIST : Miwo
COUNTRY : China
MEDIUM : Mixed Media and Collage

TITLE : Magic box
ARTIST : Miwo
COUNTRY : China
MEDIUM : Mixed Media

244

TITLE : D3zin3rs
ARTIST : Danny Teo
COUNTRY : Singapore
MEDIUM : Mixed Media and Collage

TITLE: Made in China
ARTIST: Song Han
COUNTRY: China
MEDIUM: Mixed Media and Collage

TITLE : Dime
ARTIST : Xu Bing
COUNTRY : China
MEDIUM : Mixed Media

TITLE	: Happy pao pao
ARTIST	: Xu Bing
COUNTRY	: China
MEDIUM	: Mixed Media

248

TITLE : Basic Poster
ARTIST : Giovanni Paletta
COUNTRY : Italy
MEDIUM : Mixed Media and Collage

TITLE	: Celebrity Religion
ARTIST	: MAKI
COUNTRY	: The Netherlands
MEDIUM	: Mixed Media and Collage

250

TITLE : Twins
ARTIST : Miwo
COUNTRY : China
MEDIUM : Mixed Media

TITLE : Monologue
ARTIST : Miwo
COUNTRY : China
MEDIUM : Mixed Media

252

TITLE : Soap
ARTIST : MAKI
COUNTRY : The Netherlands
MEDIUM : Mixed Media and Collage

in de volgende aflevering ga je er aan!
IK HOU VAN JE!!!!
Liefde
VREEMD GAAN
SSST
JANUARI

Contacts

A Moxilin	46002573@qq.com
Ai Tatebayashi	ai@miniai.com
Blessing Ear	blessingear@gmail.com
Brian Taylor	theape@thelittlechimpsociety.com
Chaos	chaos@chengchangimage.com
Danny Teo	danny@d3zin3.net
Driv	driv@robonut.com
Feng Jie	fj1982@eyou.com
Giovanni Paletta	me@krghettojuice.com
Gustavo Torres & Clara Luzian	info@bkrstudio.com.ar
Haruki Higashi	http://www.loworks.org
He Chuan	273816681@qq.com
Heng Lan	776379283@qq.com
Ippei Gyoubu	mail@gyoubu.com
Irana Douer	teafromchina@gmail.com
Julio Rölle	sfelix@eurocult.org
Ken Garduno	imback1028@ca.rr.com
Lee Zhuoyan	rvmagazine@gmail.com
Leonor Morais	mail@leonormorais.com
Li jinru	lijinru@126.com
Liangliang LIU	ulababa@hotmail.com
Lin Xupan	linxupan@163.com
Liu Wei	happy_eva40@hotmail.comp
Liz Amini-Holmes	liz@lunavilla.com
Lodewyk M. Barkhuizen	lodewyk@pleasecontrolme.co.za
Lucas Temby	webmaster@robotswillkill.com
MAKI	info@makimaki.nl
Manuel Larino	manuel@mlarino.com
Marie-Chantale Turgeon	m-c@mcturgeon.com
Mark Verhaagen	mark@markverhaagen.com

Mclelun	mclelun@gmail.com
Meni Tzima	http://www.yupyland.com
Michael Foster	info@fosterscafe.com
Miwo	hancy_ww@163.com
Nate Smith	nate@natesdesign.com
Nie Peng	op010@163.com
Nuansedipian	bohe_3016@163.com
Pi Jiupaopao	sl7884@163.com
Paulo Arraiano	mail@pauloarraiaon.com
Philipp Jordan	stefan@from-the-hill.nl
Postgal.com	ask@doll.com
Qian Qian	info@q2design.com
Qiuqiu	qiutiandeqiu@hotmail.com
Ray Jones	ray@jonesray.com
Róth Anikó	info@rothaniko.hu
Satata	satata59@163.com
Serge Seidlitz	info@debutart.com
Shi Wuxuan	loseverything@hotmail.com
Shin Eun-mi	shinem78@hotmail.com
Shiraz Fuman	shirazfuman@yahoo.com
Song Han	songsongbox@126.com
Steve Stone	lemon.soul@ntlworld.com
Undoboy	contact@undoboy.com
Wang Peng	info@stir-art.com
Wu Yanbing	dblagecake@hotmail.com
Xu Bing	designkids@tom.com
Yeji Yun	seeouterspace@gmail.com
Yu Lin	yuyu444@163.com
Yuhoo	liliquan_512@163.com
Zhou Yijun	mos0910@hotmail.com
Cutting Edge Design Studio	

Acknowledgements

Thank you to all the people who responded so positively to the call for entries for this book and who sent materials from around the world. Thanks also to the designers and illustrators who not only designed illustrations specially for this book but who gave immeasurable encouragement and support: Pi Jiupaopao, Qiu Qiu, Li Junru, Yuhoo.

Sincere thanks also to :editor Wu of http://www.chinavisual.com